"Mom, I'm Gay"

Revised and Expanded Edition

"Mom, I'm Gay"

Loving Your LGBTQ Child and Strengthening Your Faith

Revised and Expanded Edition

SUSAN COTTRELL

WESTMINSTER
JOHN KNOX PRESS
LOUISVILLE · KENTUCKY

© 2016 Westminster John Knox Press

© 2014, 2016 Susan Cottrell

First edition published as *"Mom, I'm Gay": Loving Your LGBTQ Child without Sacrificing Your Faith* (Austin, TX: FreedHearts Inc., 2013).

Revised and Expanded Edition
Published by Westminster John Knox Press
Louisville, Kentucky

16 17 18 19 20 21 22 23 24 25—10 9 8 7 6 5 4 3 2 1

Scripture quotations are from the New Revised Standard Version of the Bible, copyright © 1989 by the Division of Christian Education of the National Council of the Churches of Christ in the U.S.A., and are used by permission.

Photo in the appendix is courtesy of Linda Robertson.

Book design by Drew Stevens
Cover design by designpointinc.com and Tanja von Ness

Library of Congress Cataloging-in-Publication Data

Names: Cottrell, Susan, author.
Title: Mom, I'm gay : loving your LGBTQ child and strengthening your faith / Susan Cottrell.
Description: Revised and Expanded Edition. | Louisville, KY : Westminster John Knox Press, 2016.
Identifiers: LCCN 2015047259 (print) | LCCN 2015049978 (ebook) | ISBN 9780664262228 (alk. paper) | ISBN 9781611646641 ()
Subjects: LCSH: Parents--Religious life. | Families--Religious aspects--Christianity. | Homosexuality--Religious aspects--Christianity. | Sexual orientation--Religious aspects--Christianity.
Classification: LCC BV4529 .C67 2016 (print) | LCC BV4529 (ebook) | DDC 261.8/35766--dc23
LC record available at http://lccn.loc.gov/2015047259

∞ The paper used in this publication meets the minimum requirements of the American National Standard for Information Sciences—Permanence of Paper for Printed Library Materials, ANSI Z39.48-1992.

Most Westminster John Knox Press books are available at special quantity discounts when purchased in bulk by corporations, organizations, and special-interest groups. For more information, please e-mail SpecialSales@wjkbooks.com.

*To all of you in the LGBTQ community who strive to be true to yourselves,
and to the family and friends who love, defend, and encourage you.
We shall overcome!*

"How many more gay people must God create until we realize that he wants them here?"
—Hawaii Representative Kaniela Ing

CONTENTS

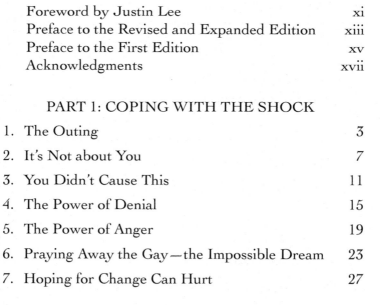

PART 5: FINDING A COMMUNITY OF SUPPORT

FOREWORD

In my years of Christian ministry work, I have heard from countless parents struggling with how to respond to their child's coming out as lesbian, gay, bisexual, or transgender.

Many of these parents are suffering from guilt, doubt, and confusion. They are committed to their faith and want to stand for what's right in God's eyes. They also love their children and would do anything to shield them from harm. But if their children make decisions they feel they can't support or if they find themselves trapped in a conflict between their church and their child, how do they strike the right balance? How do they show unconditional love without betraying their convictions?

In my own writings and ministry, I have sought to help parents grapple with these questions as Christians—but I am not a parent.

Other books have been written specifically for parents from a parent's perspective—but without a Christian focus.

Now, Susan Cottrell offers us a book from a Christian parent's perspective, in what will surely be an oasis in the desert for so many parents.

In this book, Susan avoids focusing on the polarizing

politics of homosexuality. This is not a book about same-sex marriage or Bible debates on sexual morality, though Susan does offer some thoughts of her own along the way. Instead, this is a book about how you can respond as a parent or loved one—knowing what you can change and what you can't and recognizing the ways your own response has the power to mend a damaged relationship or push your child away forever.

You may find, as you read, that Susan draws some conclusions you don't agree with. That's okay; I encourage you to keep reading anyway. Ultimately, even if you don't come to the same conclusions Susan has come to, I think you'll find much to appreciate in her approach, along with many important reminders about God's supremacy in all things.

Whoever you are, whatever you are going through right now, know that you are not alone. Many others have been down this road before, and many others are going through it alongside you.

I pray that this one mother's words offer you peace, courage, and a renewed sense of hope in an otherwise turbulent time. And I pray that God will guide and comfort you in your journey, bringing blessings you never expected out of even the darkest nights of your soul.

Justin Lee,
Executive Director,
The Gay Christian Network

PREFACE TO THE REVISED
AND EXPANDED EDITION

A WORD OF LOVE

I took my laptop with me to the kitchen for a lunch break from writing this book—I like to enjoy *TED Talks* as I cook—and today it was "10 Most Inspirational Ads." It was ad number eight, I think, that got me. I won't do it justice here but essentially: the little boy was caught stealing medicine for his mother, but a kind man gave him a break, paying for the meds and giving him soup as well—then thirty years later when that man ended up in the hospital, the boy turned out to be the doctor and so was able to forgive the insurmountable hospital debt. On the bill, he wrote: "All expenses paid 30 years ago with three packs of painkillers and a bag of veggie soup." You've seen the kind.

Suddenly, I wept. I turned off the burner under my leftover fajitas and let the tears fall, deeply moved by the profound and inherent kindness of which human beings are capable. I wept for how often people in this world need a hand to pull them up (like the little boy stealing the pain meds), need a very large break (like the man facing the hospital bill), need simple kindness (like the LGBTQ community and their families).

I wept at how many LGBTQ people need bread, but

their families give them a stone—or worse, a snake (Matt. 7:9–11).

Kindness is woefully under-expressed in our human family, yet kindness changes hearts.

I published the first edition of *"Mom, I'm Gay"* in January 2014, compelled to help terrified parents navigate the treacherous waters—societal, family, and church—that they suddenly faced because they had an LGBTQ child. I knew how disoriented these parents were, and I longed to help them—and especially *their kids*. I knew that to help the parents was to help the kids (of any age), and these kids have stolen my heart.

In these two-and-a-half years, much has changed. The Supreme Court has made marriage equality the law of the land. Many places now warmly welcome LGBTQ people. But in many ways, nothing has changed. The law still sanctions housing and workplace discrimination. Too many parents still live in terror of "homosexuality" and respond viciously to their own children. Parents who *embrace* their gay kids are still vilified.

Unkindness and rejection are perpetuated in God's name.

I fervently hope that this revised and expanded version of *"Mom, I'm Gay"* will continue to comfort both parents and their LGBTQ children, help put their fears to rest, and help revitalize them to this amazing life they have been given.

With love,
Susan

PREFACE TO
THE FIRST EDITION

A WORD OF HOPE

When our daughter first told us she was attracted to women, we were shocked. The usual questions flooded us: What would this mean for her life? Would she be safe? Would she ever have children? We had no idea what lay ahead.

But here's the realization that smacked us: we were now the "others." Whether we shared this information or not (we thought we would *not*), the church was no longer our home. In our twenty-plus years at wonderful, "grace-based" churches, we had not seen one *out* gay person, nor one family standing in support of their gay loved one.

One year later, our youngest daughter came out as well. I always joke that when the second child comes out, you as a parent immediately think: "Okay, it *is* us!" But in the years that followed, we realized that no, it was *not* us. It was who they were, and we were simply the safe place for them to come out.

So here we were with our beloved queer daughters on one hand, and the church teaching *conditional* acceptance on the other. We dearly love our Jesus who retrieved us from more perils than we can articulate. We also knew we would give our daughters only the unconditional, all-embracing love Jesus showed to the very farthest outcast—like us. If the church would make us believe that unconditional love was somehow a compromise of our faith, it was that teaching that needed to be examined. Not Jesus, and certainly not our parental love.

The church veneer had begun to crack prior to our daughter's revelation. Pastor worship, sin management, rules-based behavior, even the disproportionate application of "discipline"—all this had eroded our faith, not in the Jesus who'd dramatically changed our lives over the decades, but in a church system becoming increasingly irrelevant to a world seeking *life*. Although much good work was being done, most of our experience was of the church's overriding focus on behavior modification; we'd already experienced this during some marital challenges when our church was startlingly unequipped to offer anything usable in our time of crisis.

Over the three years that followed our daughter's revelation, we met many Christian parents of gay kids, and we realized we were not the only ones to see that the emperor had no clothes. I believe that God is shaking the church until what's left is the unshakable: *God*. I believe God is shifting the attention from behavior modification to the profound, transformative, life of the Spirit. That is where our hope lies.

Our primary job is to love God and love others, and let God take care of everything else. We can have more peace than we ever knew possible, and joy beyond our wildest dreams, as our children flourish in God's inexhaustible love for them. I hope you will join me on this quest!

Susan

ACKNOWLEDGMENTS

Thank you, wonderful God, for flinging me far from my comfort zone into a great and wild adventure. Thank you for the amazing LGBTQ friends you've given me on this journey. Thank you for families who have shown Christ's love to their gay children, actively fighting through a homophobic culture and church to do it. Thank you for the many allies who have thrown off their own reputations in favor of loving as Christ loves. Thank you for inviting me to follow your Spirit, not an ideology.

I lift this work in my hands and say, "Here, this is for you. Because you love me so."

Thank you also to Linda Robertson and all the moms in our moms' group.

Thank you to my beautiful children for your authenticity, endless love, and profound courage.

And finally, thank you to my wonderful lifelong partner, Rob, who has made this whole journey beautiful. I will love you in all ways and for always.

PART 1

COPING WITH THE SHOCK

CHAPTER 1

THE OUTING

Easter Sunday night, we sat down to watch a movie. Anthony said, "Mom, I have to tell you something." I thought, "He got a girl pregnant; he asked a girl to marry him." . . . Ha ha. He said, "Mom, I am gay." I looked at him and said, "What?"' He said, "I am gay." I thought someone stopped my world and tore my guts out and handed them to me. Instantly I thought, "You ruined MY Easter weekend . . . how dare you." I asked him, "Are you sure?" Now I realize how stupid that question was. I realized it was wrong as soon as I said it. It was a nightmare. He went to bed. Needless to say, I didn't sleep. I threw up all night."

—Patricia

"Mom, I'm gay."
You want to shove those words back in the box and put the lid on. Your child is gay. Or bisexual. Or questioning. You never saw this coming (or maybe you did). It was not what you had in mind, and it may go against everything you believe. You instantly wonder where you went wrong.

This book is a primer to help you through the process when your child (niece, grandson, sibling, or any other loved one) comes out.

Texas couple Amy and Jen (age twenty-two) had already professed their love for each other before they told their families. Amy had grown up Southern Baptist, with all its admonitions against homosexuality. She was working in a national Christian ministry, and her job agreement included an undefined clause about "moral behavior" expected of all employees.

Jen's parents were liberal, agnostic ex-hippies. Naturally, Jen and Amy told Jen's parents first, to gain the support needed to face Amy's parents.

But Jen's liberal parents went ballistic. Jen's mom called Amy's workplace and got her fired. She called friends and relatives. Then she told Jen she never wanted to see her again.

Amy's parents turned out to be kind and loving, and they actually worked to restore the damage Jen's parents had caused with others.

Parents (aunts, uncles, grandparents) have a choice of how to respond to their loved one's coming out. I write this book to show you that you have a choice and the enormous impact your choice can make on your relationship with your child, as well as on your child's future. I use "parent" and "child" throughout for easier reading, but this book is for anyone with an LGBTQ (Lesbian, Gay, Bisexual, Transgender, Queer, or Questioning) loved one. Certainly when it's possible, a parent's acceptance is without equal. But when it's not, another caring relative or friend can make a great difference as well.

My heart breaks for the many families in turmoil, trying to reconcile their faith with their love for the child—especially as that despair is unnecessary. Jesus' response to humanity is completely different from the fracturing response we see in too much of the church and the community.

To many parents, Christian or not, a child's "outing" is

not good news, and you may find yourself searching your soul for answers. You want to know how to deal with this revelation. My husband and I were in your shoes six years ago. As we wrestled with all our questions and fears, I started FreedHearts, a blog to help reconcile the love of Christ with the LGBTQ community, families, and friends. Because this terrible chasm simply does not have to be.

FreedHearts (www.freedhearts.org) has grown into a ministry to the Christian LGBTQ community, Christian parents, and all Christians willing to engage in meaningful conversation about two great issues:

1. The great disparity between the call of Christ to love and embrace in contrast to Christians' generally unloving response to the LGBTQ community.
2. The question, is homosexuality a sin? Given all the interpretation and lived experience involved, it's an important question.

These are not questions you need to wrestle with immediately. Our focus right now is helping you deal with the shock you may be feeling and guide you in a loving response to your child. I encourage you to set aside what you already know (or think you know) on the moral and cultural issues surrounding homosexuality and ask God to show you afresh what is in store for you. If you are a Christian, you need God's personal revelation now more than ever. Whether you end up supporting same-sex marriage and relationships (what is known as "Side A" in the gay Christian community) or continue to believe those relationships are sinful ("Side B"), something much bigger and more foundational is at stake here: *How are you called to respond to your beloved son or daughter?* That is the essence of this journey.

FreedHearts Work

This section at each chapter's end offers questions to ponder along the way. My hope is to guide you through this maze of confusion, past some of the biggest dangers, to help you find your way to freedom and wholeness.

Describe what happened when your child came out. Did they tell you or did you find out? What were the circumstances? Were you shocked, or did you have an idea? What was your response?

CHAPTER 2

IT'S NOT ABOUT YOU

Oh, I said such horrible things. I asked him how he could do this to us, how could he disappoint us like this. It was all about us. I'm ashamed even to think of it. But I finally realized (in prayer) that I was being as selfish as the day is long. He was the one having to bear all this, not me. Now I consider it an honor to defend my gay son.

—Colleen

So often when our children come out, we think it's about us: Where did I go wrong? How could this have happened? What can I do to fix it?

No matter how you view gayness in general—even if you heartily embrace your gay brother or lesbian neighbor—to hear your own son or daughter say they are gay can knock you back. When you become a parent, you know to expect the unexpected. But nothing can prepare you to hear that your beloved child is gay. This is the child you have cradled, spoon-fed mashed bananas, and imagined in a beautiful future. How could this be? What will people say? What does the future hold? You can't even get your head around it.

News of your child's orientation opens a Pandora's box

of emotions. Anger, fear, hurt, blame, guilt, denial. You want to shove it all back in and close the lid tight. You might accuse your child. Or try to talk some sense into them. Or cajole. Or threaten. None of this does any good, of course—it only wounds. But what other options do you have? Just to talk about options implies that somehow our child's direction is up to us—that we can take some action to steer this ship.

Instead, we need to understand some basics.

This is not something your child did to you. They did not "choose gayness" to rebel against you, get back at you, or make your life miserable. In fact, it really has nothing do with you. You did not cause it, and it's not a failure on your part. Think about it: Would your child *choose* to risk being shunned by their Christian family, bullied by peers, and ostracized by their community? Think back now on when you chose to be straight. You see what I mean? You didn't choose; it just was.

Assimilating this news about your child will require you to sort out what is yours and what is not. I hope to help you embrace your issues wholeheartedly and leave your child's issues with your child.

How do you handle your own feelings and also accept your child? How do you love them unconditionally, despite intense pressure to "hold them accountable" (whatever that means)? You may think having an LGBTQ son or daughter is the end of the world. It's not. This is the same child you loved unconditionally five minutes before they came out.

If your expectations lie shattered at your feet, then they are *your* expectations. Let God replace *your* vision for your child with *God's*. As a younger Christian, I'd been taught that homosexuality was a sin. I believed that trauma somewhere in someone's past caused it, even if they didn't remember it. To my surprise, God completely shifted my understanding. God revealed to me the many people who had great childhoods and yet are still gay and reminded me of the many people with traumatic childhoods who are still straight. Studies show no correlation between childhood trauma and being gay. Take some time to talk with God about your questions and listen for God to speak truth to you. You may be surprised.

New and unusual circumstances can draw from us new and unusual responses. Let your loved one's coming out stir up a love response beyond what you could have possibly imagined. Many parents feel instantaneous fear when their child comes out — fear for what lies ahead, not only for their child but also for themselves. Rather than trying to talk your child out of what they're telling you, you can decide to be their biggest ally. Instead of pushing you into fear, let this disclosure bring forth the protective mama bear you didn't know was in you. (This mama bear lives in both mom *and* dad.) The many parents in our FreedHearts groups have all had to learn this — but we have learned it.

We may fear for ourselves, wondering, "What will the neighbors say?" or "What will our church say?" While those responses may be understandable, choose to set them aside. Your child has taken a big step to talk to you. They were hoping you would listen and respond to them about *their* life. They did not anticipate the need to please *your* friends, *your* extended family, the pastor, and all the busybodies you know. Don't let this undue burden fall on your child.

FreedHearts Work

Look back on your initial response to your child's coming out. What were your first thoughts? Talk about your fear, anger, shock, and other emotions.

As you think about that, how much of this had to do with you versus having to do with your child? This can be painful to look at, I know. Don't be ashamed as you discover the parts of your response that were all about you.

CHAPTER 3

YOU DIDN'T CAUSE THIS

My son is gay. To constantly wonder how I, as his dad, might have caused this is idolatry. Who do I think I am to have messed up so badly that I created something even God couldn't change? That is ludicrous.

— Greg

The first thought that pops into many parents' minds is, "How did I cause this?" It's simply been the party line to believe that some environmental factor, parenting mistakes, or trauma (named or unnamed) is somehow the cause. Many parents feel *certain* of this. We wrestle with guilt, anger, and fear. We rack our brains and search our hearts to sort out where we went wrong. And we finally come to realize beyond a doubt that our child was born this way. Sometimes this fact is obvious, and sometimes parents see the signs only in retrospect.

Parents love to take credit, if only privately, for their children's accomplishments. And in the dark of night, they also blame themselves for their children's (perceived) failures. Parents often unwittingly see their children as extensions of themselves.

But that's looking in the wrong place. Parents, and

Christian parents especially, can become enmeshed in their children's lives. We can view them as a blank slate, and if we draw the best picture in the right colors, all will turn out well. But parenting has *never* worked that way.

Kate and Jeff had suspected that one of their sons was gay, and they came to peace pretty quickly with his coming out. But when their daughter came out, Kate (who knew before her husband did) was a complete wreck. She came to me torn up thinking she had caused her daughter to be gay. I asked her to ask God if she had caused it. (I knew the answer, but she needed to learn it for herself.) She prayed but didn't hear anything. "All I get is the memory of our son Dave being so afraid that he had caused his brother to be gay. It broke my heart." I waited.

"Do you see the connection?" I asked. "Do you think perhaps your blaming yourself is just as farfetched as Dave blaming himself? I think God is telling you the same thing—you did not cause her to be gay any more than Dave caused his brother to be gay." Peace settled on her as she rested assured that indeed she had not caused this.

Parents have a humongous influence over their children, certainly. God *sets kids up* with parents to guide and protect them. Parents might have provided unique opportunities for a child who is now a doctor or helped another avert a path of danger. But they cannot bring about what is not there. Seriously.

You could never have turned that child into a doctor if it hadn't come from within her—not without serious collateral damage. How many kids have been herded along a life path that did not fit them? Aaron had no option from his father but to become a lawyer. And he did. But he eventually left law because he hated it.

On the other hand, some kids (like me) spent afternoons unattended in the homes of neighbor kids who did serious drugs, yet escaped unscathed. I felt that God totally protected me, along with many others.

I'm not saying to abdicate your parental responsibilities, only that you are not nearly as in control as you think you are. This can be a brutal realization—followed by deep relief—to see ultimately how little control we have over our kids. Unfortunately, surrendering our notion of control is especially difficult because of decades of false information that has been propagated in the media.

When Jerry Falwell founded the Moral Majority in the '70s, he began a movement that the Religious Right and radio/TV broadcasts such as Focus on the Family picked up. They attributed (blamed) gayness on a distant father or overbearing mother. Studies do not support such claims—they are simply untrue, no matter how many times they've been repeated—yet those ideas have seeped deeply into our mind-set over the years and caused incalculable damage.

Fortunately, we now have a new generation that no longer believes this, though we still experience those repercussions when parents blame themselves, or their child, for being gay. *Jettison those beliefs,* no matter where you heard them and no matter how long you've had them.

You may have to go to the mat on this, in soul-searching and prayer, to come to peace that this is not your "fault." You may have preferred your child *not* be gay, or transgender, but nothing you did or didn't do made your child that way. Please take it from those who have realized through long, hard struggle that your child's orientation was there all along, and that you had nothing to do with it.

FreedHearts Work

Do you believe that you, your spouse, or some factor from childhood caused this? Why or why not? Consider asking

God to show you if that is true or not. Ask God to give you an image of what you think may have caused this in your child. Then whatever incident(s) you recall, ask God if this is why your child is LGBTQ. (I'm here to say no, it's not, but you may need to find this out for yourself.)

CHAPTER 4

THE POWER OF DENIAL

I think my sisters want to be supportive, I think they just don't know how.

—Beth

For a child to come out often elicits a deluge of emotions in the family. Parents constantly tell me about the flood of conflicting emotions they do not feel equipped to deal with.

Emotions are an ingenious system of alerts that enable us to experience and assimilate our environment. *Denial*—and its more intense form, *shock*—allow us to set aside circumstances that would otherwise overwhelm us, or that we don't understand, until we are better situated to deal with them. *Anger*—and the more primary *fear*—alert us that something is wrong and prepare us to take helpful action. *Sadness* helps us experience and grieve loss and pain. *Happiness* enables us to experience joy and then register those moments into our long-term memory. Denial is often a first big hurdle to overcome when faced with the news of your child's sexuality.

As human beings constantly sort and order and make sense of their world, denial comes in quite handy. When something difficult occurs we can set it aside, like a puzzle piece that doesn't fit, until we see the picture more clearly and can more easily find its place. Perhaps we believe (and have been taught) that "good Christian families" don't have LGBTQ kids. So when our daughter tells us she's bisexual, we have a hard time finding where that fits next to the picture we thought was in front of us. Denial gives us a minute to reexamine our understanding and let a different picture emerge instead.

One young man talked about his father's reaction when the son came out. The father said, "You are not gay. If you were gay, that would mean I am a bad father, and I'm not a bad father." This dad found it easier to *deny* his son's experience than to reexamine his belief about *why* sons are gay (the father's fault) or himself as a "bad father." This denial, or *cognitive dissonance*, appears in many forms. Severing relationship with your child and calling it love; denying people civil liberties and calling it religious freedom; throwing people out of church and calling it discipline—these are only a few of the ways we use denial to engage in the most unlovely and un-Christlike behavior.

Given the power of denial to help us retain what we already believe, it's no surprise that many families never get past their denial. To reexamine deeply held beliefs, and to admit that we or our beliefs might be wrong, requires great courage. We love to quote John 15:13: "No one has greater love than this, to lay down one's life for one's friends," but for all our talk about self-sacrifice, we won't even lay down our comfort and confidence. To follow Jesus is to surrender to the process—as he did on the cross. Lay down your rights and let God guide you to the other side.

Think of denial as a credit card: it will help get you what you want now but eventually you must pay it off. When you deny a reality, such as your child's orientation or identity, you buy time, but the longer you let it go, the more interest you pay. If your beloved spouse dies suddenly in a car crash, denial or shock can help you survive, but eventually you must come to terms with it.

If you push off accepting your son as transgender, you fracture your relationship. That is a crushing (and completely unchristian) blow to someone whom *you are called as a parent to love unconditionally*. In the end, ongoing denial appeases only you but places a crushing weight on those whose reality you deny.

Let me encourage you (put courage into you) to embrace your child and set aside the pieces you don't understand. If you're worried about what God will think of you, just cling mightily to the first and foremost command to *love*, love with all your heart, and let God reveal and heal the rest. Heal the foundational relationships God has given you, and the rest will take care of itself. I promise.

FreedHearts Work

Many Christians have been taught that emotions are unpredictable and unsafe, so they are afraid to experience the full range of their emotions. But God gave us emotions to help us navigate a vast world more richly and safely. Jesus wept, yelled in anger, felt sad, was moved to compassion, and grieved. We can too. Identify your array of emotions surrounding your LGBTQ child. How has denial played a role in your response?

CHAPTER 5

THE POWER OF ANGER

My parents get so angry when things don't go their way—yelling, slamming things. It's awful. I can't wait to get out of here.

—Casey

*A*nger is a like a notification that something is not as it should be . . . or as we *think* it should be. If we believe that being LGBTQ is reprehensible, we understandably get *angry* when our child turns out to be exactly that. I really do understand that. We may lash out at our child for "doing this to us." But please hear me when I say that such anger is misplaced. You may well be angry that now you must look at this "issue" differently. You can no longer ignore the cognitive dissonance about the *fact* of LGBTQ people. You can no longer pretend it is "those people out there."

The purpose of anger is to notify us that something is not right *in order to spur us into helpful action.* Anger can motivate us to stop a bully from beating someone up or to work against sex trafficking. Anger can make us finally stand up to an abusive spouse or to take the kids and leave. But we must direct anger into the proper channel. However naturally anger at your child wells up, it will not help. It only presses them further to change or suppress something they already spent sleepless nights and countless tears *trying* to change and suppress. Instead, let your anger press you to seek out better understanding.

As parents in our FreedHearts groups have availed themselves to new information and surrendered to a new journey, they generally find their anger is not really at their child but at family and fair-weather friends who abandoned them. They discover their anger at faulty spiritual teachings that force them to choose between their church community *and their child.* Or God and their child. Aren't we as parents right to be angry about this? This is definitely a signal that something is wrong.

Let it be righteous anger by using it to effect positive change: How unrighteous is it that our LGBTQ youth are driven from their safe communities, youth groups, and homes? Let your righteous anger motivate you to speak to church leaders about the unsafe place they have created for our LGBTQ youth.

Also, don't be afraid to express your anger at God for giving you an LGBTQ child—God already knows it's there, so to deny your anger at God only allows it to fester like an infection. Better to clear the air and get it all out there. Only then will you truly be free of it. Anger at God is actually productive because it pushes you to allow yourself to reexamine inadequate understanding and to grow past it. That can only be a good thing.

FreedHearts Work

Don't be afraid that God is unable to handle your grief or fear or sadness or guilt or shame. A God who cannot handle that is no God. Instead, let it all go, express it, and ask God for comfort and the courage to face your child's reality with an open heart.

How have you experienced anger? How has it motivated you or could it motivate you to positive action? Try to pinpoint your fear and what you are really afraid of. To identify that specifically can help relieve the tensions of it.

CHAPTER 6

PRAYING AWAY THE GAY —
THE IMPOSSIBLE DREAM

I had a lot of thoughts about wishing he'd just try to like girls,
believing his orientation was my fault, etc. —but thank God the
only voice I allowed out of my mouth was the one that took him
seriously, the one I'd have wanted to hear if I were in his shoes.

—Rick

Tanya came to our group two years ago, a complete
wreck. She wanted to join us and find camaraderie
among moms who had been there, but she couldn't let go
of her attempts to change her son. She really believed she
could do it. The rest of us knew better.

Our group meets people where they are and helps them
through. We love everyone who comes to us, and we include
all who are sorting through having an LGBTQ child. But
it is hard to work with parents who actively seek to change
their child. You see, that's how Linda lost her son. [1]

Linda and her husband, Rob, believed that if they just
did it right, just got him focused on Jesus, just prayed
enough, he would become straight. They did everything

the church community counseled. Tragically, that only taught him to hate himself, and they lost him.

Two years later, Tanya came back. She had been on quite a journey in that time, and one of our moms had stayed in touch with her, saying, "I think she's going to need us." Indeed, she did, and now she is in a restored relationship with her gay son and delighted in who he is.

It seems the nearly universal response when someone comes out (to their family or just to themselves) is to beg and plead that God would take away the same-sex attraction. Like the stages of grief after a death, denial and anger are followed by bargaining. If praying, wishing, and believing meant that homosexuality would not visit our homes, we wouldn't see it popping up everywhere. But praying, wishing, and believing will not make your child straight. I have heard countless stories of people who prayed without ceasing, and nothing changed.

Exodus International has led the way in so-called "reorientation therapy" but to no avail. On "Our America with Lisa Ling—Special Report: God and Gays," Navy Veteran Sean Sala told Exodus President Alan Chambers of his time in a pit of deep despair and anger after pleading with God to change his same-sex attractions. Sean woke up one morning so desperate that he went to get the gun his friend kept loaded in his gun closet. Just the thought of killing himself made him feel like he was "opening a Christmas present." He stood there praying the same prayer he had prayed a million times: "God, why will you not change me?" Then, Sean said, "I can't describe it but something from the outside told me not to take my life and I said, 'God, why won't you change me?' and it said to me, "Because there is nothing I need to change about you.'"[2]

I have heard similar stories several times from men and women who pled with God to change them and finally heard, "I made you this way." What peace it brings to know that God created you as you are.

Even so, some still claim that a gay sexual orientation needs to be changed — and that such change is possible. Has anyone prayed themselves straight? The truth is that I don't know a single story like that, although I know some who have suppressed themselves. But we know that countless LGBTQ people have prayed, done everything right, followed every suggestion, gone to support groups, and poured themselves wholeheartedly into being straight, only to sink into self-loathing when the promised change didn't come.

On the contrary, the thirty-seven-year experiment that was Exodus International demonstrated that so-called "ex-gay" or "reparative therapy" programs do not "reorient" people. They have caused horrific conflict and self-loathing for countless hopefuls, including men who "stepped out in faith" to marry a woman, hoping attraction would come. It never did . . . and it caused tremendous collateral damage.

Please don't put that weight on your child, to ask for a change God does not intend to make. Your child does not deserve this. If you do, to borrow the wonderful words of the wise Gamaliel in Acts 5:39, "you may even be found fighting against God!"

Your time is best spent seeking God's plan instead of yours and peacefully surrendering to the path God really does have for you.

Let God use this unexpected situation with your child to show you something new. God is always doing something and changing us — conforming us to our innate divine image.

FreedHearts Work

Are you harboring the hope that God will change your child's orientation? (It's okay to be honest. Believe me, you're not the only one who hopes for change for their child.) Have you asked whether that is what God wants? Or are you asking because it's what *you* want? Don't let fear run away with you. Ask God to show you.

Are you willing to place your child and this whole situation in God's hands? Ask God to show you anything you need to see about your child regarding the possibility for change. Surrender all of that, and ask God to help you when you forget you surrendered it.

CHAPTER 7

HOPING FOR CHANGE CAN HURT

Worst thing I said to Alex: "I think there are workshops that can help you if you are gay" (he had just told me that he didn't know, because that is what I wanted to hear). There was fear in his eyes, and he asked if I would make him do it. I said, "No, it is just a suggestion." Believe me I had no idea what I was talking about. This was one reason it took him five years to tell us that he was gay.

—Debby

Many years ago, long before I started FreedHearts, long before our daughters came out, I asked my mentor what her answer was for people who are gay. If she thought gay relationships are wrong, what did she suggest? She suggested Exodus International because they were "phenomenal at leading people out of the homosexual lifestyle." It sounded pretty doubtful to me, to be honest, because I didn't really think being gay could change. My childhood neighbor and my best (guy) friend in high school were both gay, and change just didn't seem possible.

If you are holding out hope that your child's orientation can be changed, please consider the harm such attempts can have on your child. Even Exodus International has repented of their efforts. In June 2013, after thirty-seven years of so-called "reparative therapy," Exodus International closed its doors. Finally, having observed the actual lived experience of attendees, Exodus leaders admitted that ex-gay therapy simply does not work, and President Alan Chambers apologized for the deep and broad damage this false hope of "reorientation" had caused the LGBTQ community.

In a panel at the Gay Christian Network conference in 2012, Chambers stated, "The majority of people that I have met, and I would say the majority meaning 99.9 percent of them, have not experienced a change in their orientation."[1] One of the original Exodus founders, Michael Bussee, and volunteer Gary Cooper are perfect examples of this, as they finally left their straight marriages and ended up together.

Later, Chambers presented an apology to the LGBTQ community upon the closing of Exodus. He said:

> I am sorry we promoted sexual orientation change efforts and reparative theories about sexual orientation that stigmatized parents. I am sorry that there were times I didn't stand up to people publicly "on my side" who called you names like sodomite — or worse.[2]

If "ex-gay therapy" were pain relief medicine, it would be off the shelves with the company defending against a class-action suit. And like a defective pain med, reparative therapy not only fails to help but can be deadly. People have been badly wounded by the false hope that if they would just pray, study, and counsel, then change can occur. But the damage that comes from that — through self-hatred and shame, through broken marriage vows made "in faith," to kids of those marriages — is incalculable. To require such change is not loving because it leaves gay people holding the bag, expected to change, even believing in faith that they have changed, and loathing themselves, sometimes to the point of suicide, when change doesn't come.

"Ex-gay" ministries get suggested as a "compassionate solution for a difficult problem," but they simply don't work. Nor are they compassionate. In fact, you may be surprised to know that so-called "reparative therapy" includes the use of porn to stimulate opposite attraction, and electric shock *to the genitals* to inhibit same-sex attraction. No wonder this is banned in some states and advocates are pushing to ban it in *all* states.

Is this the Christlike response, the compassionate solution Christians have to offer? No.

The compassionate solution is to surrender to God and not try to make people fit what will keep your worldview intact. Real compassion means to face what is, seek to understand what your child has gone through and is still going through, and respond with love.

FreedHearts Work

Hope for change can continue to flail around in us, long after we have accepted our child's orientation. It may show up in one of two ways:

1. as unresolved grief for loss of the future you had envisioned for your child. If that is the case, recognize your loss, express it, and grieve it.
2. as active hope, which you communicate to your child whether you mean to or not. Even a "secret hope" for change still reads as incomplete acceptance, which has a deleterious affect on your family relationships. In this case, ask God to show you if it is not to be.

(Bear in mind the countless testimonies of those who begged and pleaded for change and did not get it.) Recognize that any change God wants to make, God will make, but prayer for change does not seem to bring change. Ask God to show you a clear picture of the damage that comes from hoping your child will do something they cannot do.

PART 2

UNDERSTANDING YOUR CHILD'S EXPERIENCE

CHAPTER 8

"YOU'RE NOT GAY, YOU'RE JUST CONFUSED"

Oh, my poor girl. I must have asked her a hundred times how she knew she was attracted to women. She was so patient with me! She just knew, and she had known since she was quite young.

—Margot

Ashley is a smart, straight young woman who has done profound work to help young women break free from Christian, male-dominated thinking. Ashley and her siblings were never allowed to disagree with their parents. Her oppressive father would say, "No, Ashley, your mom is not wrong; you're just confused." Ashley learned to doubt herself and her perceptions. As an adult, she had to track down the source of that doubt as coming from her *parents' interpretation* of her thoughts, not the *reality* of her thoughts. It took some work, but now Ashley knows she is not at all confused—she just sometimes disagrees.

When you discover your child's orientation, your instinct is to doubt, deny, question—especially if it comes out of the blue. You have had no time to process it. But realize that it's not news to your child. By the time your child comes out to you, they have probably lived with this for some time and processed it quite a bit. I mean, just think about it. Their first inklings of same-sex attraction startled them. Scared them. They had to discover how true it was. They had to watch other young teens grow into puberty and realize they weren't developing the same feelings. Perhaps they dated the opposite gender to see if passion might develop, yet none did. They denied it, praying this was not true about them. Every LGBTQ person I know—especially those from a faith background—has prayed that prayer.

By the time your child comes out to you, they are pretty sure of what they're saying. They did not rush out to tell you first thing. When you found yourself attracted to someone as a preteen, did you rush off to tell your parents? Probably not. Add to that the jarring realization that *these are same-gender attractions*—which are almost always disconcerting and require time to process and be sure about before disclosing. By the time your child comes out to you, they know what they are talking about.

Do not ask them if they are sure, if maybe they want to take a little time and see what happens. Instead, consider the journey they have been through. You might ask things like, "When did you know?" "How long have you felt this way?" But don't let your burden become their burden. Instead, tell them you are grateful that they are including you in their journey and that they no longer have to go through this alone. Even if they are saying they are not sure, that's okay. This is still the life-giving response.

Then give yourself time to process. By all means. You will need to work through your own wave of emotions. Seek information, a trusted friend, whomever or whatever you need to help you assimilate this. Your emotions will affect your child, so you will want to discuss some things with them. They may invite you to share your thinking, and they may even help you through it. But it is not their job. Just as you wouldn't work out marital issues through your child (even though emotions about your marriage affect them), don't process all your emotions about your child's orientation with them.

Jeanie was so shocked when her son came out to her that she wrote him a vitriolic letter. "How could you do this? You're an idiot! You're selfish, and you're destroying our family." Fortunately, she confided to a friend who convinced her not to send it. Jeanie is glad she heeded that wise counsel. It took some years, but she has now come to terms with her son's sexuality and completely accepts the situation. She knows beyond any doubt that her son did not choose to be gay any more than *she* chose to be straight.

Do not throw your Bible at your child in a blind panic. Instead, take those verses that trouble you, along with what you've internalized from church, *and ask God about it.* Let God reveal God's heart on this. As I walked through this issue, God addressed my doubts specifically and lovingly, showing me that none of the biblical writers had any concept of a loving same-sex relationship—the Bible addresses only sex with slave boys, rape, and temple idol practices. Remember that the Spirit will lead us in all truth (John 16:13). As you hear truth, you will find yourself filled with love and peace for your child, and for the LGBTQ community as a whole. That is when you know you are hearing the very heart of God.

FreedHearts Work

Describe what you know about your child's journey of discovery. How long did they know before they told you? Who else did they tell? Talk about how you felt that they had kept this secret: Heartbroken? Betrayed? Wondering what else you don't know? Wondering if they really are sure? Talk about those feelings with your partner or another trusted friend, knowing that they're just feelings, and it's okay to have them.

CHAPTER 9

TERRIFIED TO TELL YOU

When Alex finally told his family, his father kicked him and threw him down the stairs. But he couldn't leave because he wasn't old enough. When he turned eighteen, he took off with nothing. No college because there was no financial aid because his parents made too much money—even though they didn't give him any. Right now he's sleeping on my sofa and working at Starbucks.

—Jules

When Emily came out to her parents, she brought them to her dorm room, so she could be on her own turf, and she said, "I have campus security on speed dial." What? Her mother, Robin, remembers feeling like she was punched in the gut. How terrible she felt that her own daughter felt she needed to secure her borders before coming out. But she knew the stories.

Like most of our LGBTQ kids, your child knew how shocked they were to discover they were different, and they know there's a good chance you'll be shocked too. Not only shocked but hostile. They have imagined you being upset, yelling at them, throwing them out, even disowning them. Believe me, these kids have heard the stories, and they are hoping their parents won't go ballistic. They've probably wondered what they'll do if they are rejected, where they'll go, how they'll move forward. They've played and replayed in their minds what their parents have *already said* about homosexuality.

The risk is real. Gay teens have been shamed, banished, threatened, beaten, and shunned. They are on the street, turned out by their parents. Some 40 percent of homeless teens in Los Angeles are gay or lesbian, 68 percent of those have experienced family rejection, and 54 percent have experienced abuse in their family. They know that once they say it, they cannot unsay it. Don't think our kids don't weigh that risk every day.[1]

The following letter from a father to his son remains viral even after several years. It represents the worst fears of the child who comes out.

James:

This is a difficult but necessary letter to write. I hope your telephone call was not to receive my blessing for the degrading of your lifestyle. I have fond memories of our times together, but that is all in the past. Don't expect any further conversations with me. No communications at all. I will not come to visit, nor do I want you in my house. You've made your choice though wrong it may be. God did not intend for this unnatural lifestyle. If you choose not to attend my funeral, my friends and family will understand. Have a good birthday and good life. No present exchanges will be accepted.

—Goodbye,
Dad

This horrifying response reveals volumes about the father who wrote it, *not* the son who received it. Even someone who considers same-sex relationships sinful has no justification from God to withdraw love like this. *None*. This stance can also inhibit the support other family members would have extended. To challenge a vehement spouse can be intimidating, no doubt, but all the more necessary, isn't it? If you are in that unfortunate position, afraid to speak up against the rejecting parent, please seek out wisdom and courage to be true to *your* heart, instead of avoiding the conflict and throwing your beloved child under the bus.

Contrast the response of James's dad above to that of Nate's dad below:

> Nate:
>
> I overheard your phone conversation with Mike last night about your plans to come out to me. The only thing I need you to plan is to bring home OJ and bread after class. I've known you were gay since you were six. I've loved you since you were born.
>
> —Dad
>
> P.S. Your mom and I think you and Mike make a cute couple.

Your child knows your response could go either way. Quite possibly your feelings lie somewhere in the middle of these two letters. You may not be as fully accepting as Nate's mom and dad, and I hope (we all hope) you are not in agreement with James' dad. Wherever you might be, I pray you can express your acceptance of your son or daughter as a person.

You may not like the sweater you received for Christmas, but you can certainly appreciate the thoughtfulness, time, and effort Aunt Mary expended to get it to you. Similarly, you can express appreciation for your child's dilemma, knowing God is able to direct them in this intensely personal area.

Perhaps the letter below can offer a place to start as you respond to your child.

> Son, the first thing I want you to be sure of is that we love you, always have, always will. We are proud of you. We admire the young man you've become. Thank you for telling us about this part of you. I can only imagine how difficult it was for you to say to your old mom and dad! You already know that homosexuality goes against our beliefs. But we are going to pray to see this from God's perspective, apart from the culture and the church. I admit we are also concerned for you — mostly because this world can be cruel and we don't want you to be hurt. Know that we will do our best to protect you. I realize you may be tempted to protect us from family and friends who disagree with homosexuality. We want you to know that you are not to concern yourself with that. That is our job as your parents. No matter what, we love you and would never do anything to hurt you.

Keep the big picture in mind. Notice that if you must mention your disagreement (though they're already aware of it), do so in a way that *owns* it instead of shoving the burden on them. Always speak from your *love* relationship.

FreedHearts Work

Take a good long look at the courage your child had to come out to you. Consider the courage it takes to stand for who you are, especially when you've fought against it, prayed against it, and denied it as long as you could, and now you choose to stand—especially when others who do not like it can make life so miserable for you because of it.

If your initial response was less than glowing, please forgive yourself. Instead, make amends with your child; ask forgiveness, if you have not yet done so. Only an enemy torments us over our mistakes—God does not. Please don't torture yourself over what has transpired. Forgive yourself, accept your child's forgiveness, and move on with the business of loving them. The time is now for a beautiful relationship with your child!

CHAPTER 10

WHAT NOT TO SAY, PART 1

All these statements make our kids feel broken, second-rate, less-than.

—Sandy

Keiko was a Japanese girl who sat next to me in sixth grade. I mentioned her over the dinner table and my father, who had served in World War II, said something casually, not maliciously, about her being a "Jap." I'd never heard the word and repeated it the next day. I was shocked when Keiko was offended. I had no intention of hurting her, and I had no idea this was an ethnic slur.

People today casually toss out remarks to and about LGBTQ people, not realizing why or even *that* they are offensive. But they are as offensive as ethnic slurs. It's easy to throw out sound bites as if they are definitive, but I would *hope* that most of us would stop saying them if we understood the impact.

Part of understanding your child's experience is to hear the things they have been told (things that perhaps even you have said) through your child's ears. Common as these phrases are, try to look at them afresh and see why they are so hurtful.

"I can't approve of 'the gay lifestyle.'"

Some words just get repeated and repeated and repeated, with no thought behind them. There is no "gay lifestyle"—just as there is no "straight lifestyle." There are just *people*, who live in a variety of ways—gay or straight—who have sex or don't have sex—gay or straight. They may be faithfully monogamous or flagrantly promiscuous—*gay or straight*. Please let me encourage you to strike this phrase from your vocabulary. It unkindly implies a dirty promiscuity—an obsession with sex. Whether you intend that or not, that is how it is heard.

"It's a choice."

Only straight people talk about the choice to be LGBTQ. Ask them when they chose to be straight. The answer, of course, is that it wasn't a choice—it just always *was*. Countless parents in our FreedHearts Moms and Dads groups will tell you, our children did not make a choice. It's just who they are.

My friend Nancy loves to say, "Not a choice, not a sin." She knows her boy inside out, she watched him grow up, and she knows he never chose to be gay. He also never endured some secret abuse that "made" him gay. Parents in the trenches can tell you: *Not a choice, not a sin.* To continue to talk about *choice* offends those who are *in* it, denies their lived experience, and says you know about them better than they do. That is no way to treat a fellow human being.

"The parts don't fit."

Anatomical arguments against homosexuality are based on the assumption that male/female is the only workable model and/or that procreation is the sole or primary goal of sexual partnership. Clearly what we hear from the LGBTQ community is, it's not. The argument for procreation is disingenuous; have you ever heard this objection when it's an old couple marrying? No one suggests we restrict marriage for those who are unable to or even simply uninterested in having children. No one even asks.

The main point of the Adam and Eve story is that the best partner for a person is another *person*, not an animal—hence the context of Adam naming all the animals and finding no suitable partner among them. Then, voilà, another human. A perfect fit. This is also the main reason (besides being generally offensive) that homosexuality is not equivalent to bestiality. To argue that two men together is equivalent to a man and a dog is really silly. As Ellen Degeneres wrote in her book *The Funny Thing Is . . .*, "That is where they go right away. These people scare me. They think *we're* weird."

"They're an abomination."
Need I really explain how this feels? It's a terrible thing to say. And it's disingenuous. No one holds up signs saying that shrimp eaters, football players, and mixed-fabric wearers are an abomination. Besides, "abomination" as it is used in the Hebrew Scriptures really means something not allowed for this time for these people—it's more like "taboo." Neither ancient Hebrews nor Jews at the time of Jesus would have expected Gentiles to adhere to these same rules, and debates in the early church clarified that Gentile Christians did not need to avoid those "abominations" like shrimp and pigskin either (see Acts 15:28–29, for example).

"They exchanged the truth for a lie."
Similarly, quoting this verse of Scripture (Rom. 1:25) is to take something entirely out of context. Paul is talking here about idol worshipers in ongoing temple sex practices. He is not talking about our children—our children have not succumbed to temple sex practices.

"I'm just telling you what the Bible clearly says. It's not me saying it, it's God."

Some people say it is the loving thing to do to tell people where they are wrong, but God loves them infinitely more than any person does, so we can trust God to speak to them directly. All we accomplish in assaulting people with Scripture is risk turning them off from listening to God at all. Just as a high-pressure salesman turns people off from being sold, so do high-pressure Christians turn people off from trusting God. If God and the Bible are so clear about it, then there is no need for you to make sure they see it. God is fairly competent without our help. Put it down and trust God.

FreedHearts Work

Can you hear how these words would be received? Can you hear how they are not neutral but harmful? Are you willing to lay them down and let God lead, let God speak on this? Are you willing to speak up when you hear these words spoken instead of letting them go? In this way we can bear one another's burdens and treat our children as we ourselves would want to be treated.

CHAPTER 11

WHAT NOT TO SAY, PART 2

When people tell me love the sinner hate the sin, I say, "Love every-one and hate your own sin!"

—Gabrielle

Love God and love others. Don't judge lest you be judged. These were important words from Jesus about how his followers were to carry on without him. I'm not sure where the life of a Christ-follower became about correcting others instead of loving others, but I suspect it's all about the human desire to be in charge. Zig Ziglar said, "Some people find fault like there's a reward for it."

Unfortunately, Christians seem to lead the way on this march, correcting each other as if that were the message of the gospel. My daughter Hannah told me she easily preferred her theater group to youth group, because in theater, she could be who she was, but in youth group, unspoken expectations just hung over her head.

Paul speaks compellingly about leaving us to hear God for ourselves, not to insist on our brothers and sisters doing it our way. Think about how your child feels when they hear these sin-focused comments from well-meaning brothers and sisters in Christ.

"Being gay is like any other sin."

This is meant to be gracious, but it's not. "Hey, everybody sins, so let's not get bent out of shape about *this* one." Even if the intent is admirable, this phrase starts with the premise that being gay is a sin, for which you will find thoughtful and well-assimilated disagreement. Realize that gay Christians have already clawed and fought and struggled their way through this question more than you could possibly imagine.

Let me explain why being gay is *not* like alcoholism, drug addiction, porn, drunk driving, or other things people say it's like. First, it is *possible* to stop addictive behavior. Second, when an alcoholic or other addict stops their addictive behavior, their life improves. They are happier, their family is happier, their work is better. All areas improve. No one seriously argues that being on a drunken bender is a good thing. *The addiction is a distortion of who someone is; being clean and sober is the authentic expression of who that person is.*

By contrast, trying to "stop being LGBTQ" leads to depression, anxiety, self-hatred, despair — need I go on? *Sexual orientation or gender identity is authentic to who someone is; it is the denial that is a distortion.* (This may be where you will disagree with me, saying that LGBTQ identity is *not* authentic, but such a claim is indefensible on many levels. Those who have not experienced this attempt to distort one's authentic self must defer to those who have.)

Finally, proof that this argument is disingenuous is that these people don't *treat* this "like any other sin." Divorced people, gossips, self-righteous people, sexually active single heterosexuals — none are singled out as LGBTQ people are singled out, none are treated the way LGBTQ people are treated. Let's just stop pretending on this one.

"Love the sinner, hate the sin."
This has become a little tagline, which, again, many people think of as kind. It is *not* kind. It's judging someone to be a sinner, and proceeding to give oneself full permission to hate that thing they've judged. Which, as it turns out, is embedded in that person's identity.

In the *Merchant of Venice*, the moneylender was in the end denied his "pound of flesh" payment, because it is impossible to remove someone's flesh and not also take blood, to which the moneylender had no claim. So too is it impossible to hate the LGBTQ part of somebody and not hate that somebody.

"Go and sin no more."
Too many people falsely believe that Jesus told people right and left to "go and sin no more." Commenters on my blog have said that repeatedly. But it is false. It is only in the Bible twice — once to a lame man (John 5), and once to the woman forgiven for adultery (John 8). That's it. The idea that "go and sin no more" is repeated throughout Scripture is completely wrong. In both cases, Jesus was speaking to specific circumstances that we do not understand. In John 5, we are left to wonder what the man had done to bring this condition upon himself, since Jesus never otherwise associated being lame with sin. To generalize that verse to mean that sin produces disability is an irresponsible reading. (Jesus makes that clear in John 9 with the man born blind.)

In the other case, Jesus addresses a woman caught in adultery and then dragged to him. If Jesus did say it (the story is not in the earliest manuscripts), he did so only after he drove away all the others from saying or doing *anything*.[1] Jesus was very clear that none of us is in a position to correct others, even those caught red-handed.

In both cases, *Jesus said it*. And he clearly forbade

anyone else to say it. Jesus did not deliver random edicts but only spoke into the existing context of real people in real situations.

Jesus has every right to say anything, to anyone. *We do not.*

Besides, *no one* goes and sins no more.

The bottom line when considering any of these offensive statements and the ideas they represent is that we must seek to understand before we seek to be understood. I had a conversation with someone recently, someone who really understands the love of Christ, but she wasn't talking about any of that—she was repeating what she'd been soaking up from some televangelist from TBN. That was a pretty harsh realization. What hope do we have if I'm talking to her, but TBN is answering back? If you sound like your pastor or FOX News or TBN, you probably are not thinking for yourself but repeating what you've heard. You're probably not seeking to understand.

It's tough to look at these statements from a new light when we have been taught otherwise for decades now. It requires a new paradigm. But to take up your cross *means* it will be hard. What's more, we owe our children that much—don't we?

FreedHearts Work

Have you made any of these comments? After reading this chapter, can you see how these comments might be received? Would you want someone to say them to you? Are you willing to shift your language around this?

CHAPTER 12

BEYOND THE BINARY

What I see from Jesus is that he doesn't speak of intersex as a result of the fall into sin. I see Jews and Christians making space for intersex members of their communities. I hear Isaiah promising eunuchs a place in God's temple — which I read as a promise of their place in the new Heaven and New Earth. If I read from Genesis to Revelation, I see God folding in more and more outsiders so that God's house can finally be a "house of prayer for all people." (It's the same passage from Isaiah 56:1–7.)

— Benjamin L. Corey[1]

There is one more Bible verse that gets recklessly thrown around in attempts to invalidate the experience and identity of LGBTQ individuals.

"God created them male and female."
Many people use Genesis 1:27 as a trump card to declare both that people can only be male or female, with nothing in between, and (especially when paired with Gen. 2:18–25) that male and female were made as complementary partners, as the only proper partnership there is. But just as God did not create every human who would ever live all in that one moment, this verse does not refer to the

full breadth of humanity. Most may be male and female, but not all.

In fact, God created some *both* male and female, and some *neither* male nor female. Some have one type of genitalia on the outside and the other on the inside. That is called *intersex*. This term refers to "a variety of conditions in which a person is born with a reproductive or sexual anatomy that doesn't seem to fit the typical definitions of female or male."[2]

If God made male and female, God also made intersex—and as Christians are fond of saying, *God did not make a mistake.* If we don't understand something, perhaps it is we who make the mistake. Megan K. DeFranza states this eloquently in her book *Sex Difference in Christian Theology: Male, Female, and Intersex in the Image of God.*

> If we look closely, I think we find broad themes—male and female, creatures of the land, creatures of the sky, creatures of the sea; night and day, but not dusk; sun, moon, and stars, but no comets. There are many creations which are simply not named in the creation accounts. Amphibians—hybrid animals that are "creatures of the sea" and "creatures of the land"—are noticeably absent and yet I have never heard a scientist who is a Christian explain their existence as one of the "results of the fall into sin."
>
> But I have heard this explanation more than I care to count to make sense of the presence of human beings who have mixed sex characteristics. Some people insist that God created humans to be male or female and anyone whose body falls somewhere in between the categories of "Adam" or "Eve" must be proof of the "fall."[3]

Sometimes even more than sexuality, gender can be complicated to understand for those of us who do not like any gray areas. We like things to fit into files we already have in our heads, because it's easy and we can go on to think about other things. We like things to make sense, and if we have never experienced otherwise, a distinct male-female "gender binary" (that is, the classification of sex and gender into two distinct, opposite, and disconnected forms of masculine and feminine) makes sense.

But in fact, gender isn't—and never was—that simple. As with orientation and other "unmentionables" throughout history, humankind has simply chosen, well, not to mention them. That humanity has begun to talk about these issues more readily in recent years does not mean they are more common, only that they're more visible.

As discussions of gender identity become more commonplace in our culture, it can be even more important to understand the difference between gender and sexuality, and your child will appreciate your efforts to understand these sometimes confusing terms.

Gender identity is not orientation; transgender does *not* mean gay. Gender identity is who you are; sexual orientation is who you love. Or, in very basic terms: gender is what's in your head, orientation is what's in your heart, and sex is what's in your pants. Sometimes, the gender one knows oneself to be inside does not match the physical anatomy one was born with—this is what it means to be transgender. Those of us whose gender and sex organs match (whether we are oriented toward the same gender, or the opposite gender, or both) are called *cisgender.*

In her *TED Talk*, Alice Dreger[4] tells the story of a young man who grew up a "regular" boy in every way. He fell in love with a young woman he had been dating. He eventually had to go to the doctor for stomach issues that would not stop. The doctor discovered that the young man had a uterus and fallopian tubes. Imagine the shock all the way around. In his case, because his external genitalia matched what was in his brain and because he was oriented to love women, he considered himself a straight, cisgendered man. But things were actually a bit more complex.

All of this can be extremely difficult for those who cite that "God created them male and female." But instead of telling others who they are or who they should be, let's allow others to tell us who they are. Let's humble ourselves to consider that God's creation is not as simple as we may have thought.

FreedHearts Work

Think about the reality of intersex people. How does their existence and experience square with the idea of gender as a solely male-female binary? Think about broader gender issues that have been questions for you. Roles you've been held to because of your gender. Tomboys and effeminate men. Trans people. Ask yourself if you might be brave enough for more fluidity on those roles.

CHAPTER 13

"HE'S WEARING A DRESS!"

I've known I was female inside since I was young, but I couldn't do anything about it. People don't get that.

— Meghan Stabler

Claudia knew her son was transgender since he was eighteen months old. He expressed himself through girls' toys and clothing. Now at eight, he understands that he is "gender-nonconforming" (GNC), and with the help of his patient parents, he has learned where he can safely dress as a girl (at home) and where his Cinderella shoes will draw ridicule (at school).

On the other hand, we have Marie, who had been severely traumatized as a baby before being adopted. She told her family she wasn't a girl but a boy. She dressed in boys' clothes and insisted on a boy's name. Why? "Because boys don't get hurt," she said. Her parents wisely allowed her to identify as a boy. After a time, she finally decided she was a girl after all.

Scenarios like Marie's do exist. But many children, like Claudia's child, adamantly insist from a very young age, that they are in the wrong body and they maintain that their entire lives. Years back, a boy wrote to Ann Landers saying he was a girl inside. To my shock at the time, she wrote back that he could make that transition when he's ready. I was horrified. *The boy just needs serious counseling,* I thought. *The boy just needs to be told he is a boy, not a girl,* I in my ignorance thought.

I now understand that some people are born with the deep sense that they are in the wrong-gendered body, and no amount of denying, cajoling, or counseling will change that. To tell your child, "You're a boy (or girl), and I don't want to hear another word," just won't cut it.

For decades, doctors have been choosing and assigning a sex to intersex babies, generally based on which genitalia seems to dominate—though many of those individuals later find that the sex the doctor assigned does not fit with their gender identity. Today, the more common practice is to postpone surgery, rather than arbitrarily assigning a gender identity that may or may not fit the child's internal identity.

If your child is questioning their gender identity, you may experience shock, denial, fear, anger, sadness, or loss. But please hear me: you did not cause this. GNC does not come from an overbearing mom or a weak dad, no matter how many times that idea is repeated. Transgender or GNC is a complex issue, and its causes are still unknown. Some theorize that it could be related to the level of hormones present in the womb, while other research indicates it could be related to brain structure.[1] While we don't understand everything about this issue, we do know that to try to dissuade your child from GNC will only sublimate their need; it will increase anxiety, not relieve it. Only by following your child's lead on gender identity will they (and you) find real peace.

Andrew Solomon, author of *Far from the Tree: Parents,*

Children, and the Search for Identity, tells this story on the radio program *The Diane Rehm Show*:

> There was one family, for instance, in which the child had been diagnosed with ADD, attachment disorder, opposi- tional defiant disorder and bipolar disorder. He was on a whole bunch of medication for all of these things. He was in constant therapy and he kept saying also, and to them sort of marginally, "oh, but I'm really a girl." And finally they decided they would let their child live for awhile as the girl he insisted he was or that she insisted she was. And when they allowed that all of the other diagnoses evaporated and it turned out that all that pain and anguish and what appeared to be mental illness was a manifestation of the frustration and anxiety caused by being forced to live in a gender that felt wrong.[2]

Imagine if you had to live as the opposite gender. *That's* what it feels like.

If your child is not cisgender but transgender, please take heart. Seek outside support so that you and your child get the support you need: local groups such as PFLAG, therapists and counselors that specialize in transgender issues, online groups and forums. They're available and so helpful. If you and your spouse can be in agreement about following your child's lead about their gender identity and expression, it's all the better for your child. If agreement is not possible, please do not sacrifice your child to keep the marital peace. Such peace will evaporate, and you will destroy your child.

You will also want to grieve the loss of your expectations for your child and for the gender you thought your child was. Allow the emotions to come. They are normal. The more deeply you express your grief, the freer you will be.

Please take heart and seek help — and trust God through it all.

FreedHearts Work

What has been your experience, if any, with transgender or gender-nonconforming issues? This might include anything from a daughter who wants short hair and boys' clothes to a son who insists he is a girl. If this has been a source of pain for you regarding your child, talk about that. How has your insight on this subject grown? Is there anything you would like to ask someone else so that you can gain better understanding?

CHAPTER 14

THE MASCULINITY MYTH

It hurt when someone suggested just because our son was "wired" differently (which he's always known), that wasn't a valid reason to be gay. That hurt because we don't want to discount what our child says. It brings out the mama bear in us. The bottom line is . . . it really doesn't matter. Ya love them anyway. Don't lose sleep over what might have been, but instead embrace them and love who they are now.

—Wanda

You may remember those ads in the backs of magazines with the big bully kicking sand in the face of the skinny guy. It was some kind of muscle-building ad. The implication was that the skinny guy was not manly enough.

Many of our sons, whether gay or straight, transgender or cisgender, have experienced bullying because they did not fit certain expectations of what a boy or a man was supposed to be. Where did this definition come from? Who defined manhood for us?

Brené Brown reveals a startling finding in her *TED Talk* on shame:

When looking at the traits associated with masculinity in

the US, the researchers identified the following: winning, emotional control, risk-taking, violence, dominance, play-boy, self-reliance, primacy of work, power over women, disdain for homosexuality, and pursuit of status.[1]

This is a serious situation. It means that to inflict shame on LGBTQ individuals is basically part of the fabric of our culture. "For men," Brown says, "there's a cultural message that promotes homophobic cruelty. If you want to be masculine in our culture, it's not enough to be straight—you must also show an outward disgust for the gay community."

This also means that many LGBTQ teens, particularly males, are vulnerable on several levels—they face bullying by males who disdain homosexuality, they must also face their own learned disdain for homosexuals, and they must face their father's internalized disdain for homosexuality. Parents must squarely recognize their own disdain and seek to dislodge it, so as not to communicate shame to their LGBTQ children, and to their gay sons in particular.

You did not form your understanding of masculinity and neither did your son. It came as part of the package of living here. Don't punish your son for not measuring up to the culture's idea of manhood. Instead, challenge the cultural idea of manhood.

Look at the broad diversity we see in men we admire: Musicians Bruno Mars, Adam Levine, John Lennon, Rod Stewart, Prince. Dancers Mikhail Baryshnikov, Fred Astaire. Athletes Michael Sam, Bruce (now Caitlyn) Jenner, Gareth Thomas. Actors Tom Hardy, Johnny Depp, Martin Short, John Malkovich, Joseph Gordon-Levitt, Zachary Quinto. Innovator Bill Gates. President Barack Obama. These men are authentic males who don't fit a narrowly defined image—caricature—of maleness.

Similarly, don't hold your daughter to a certain view of women. Instead, challenge that view. You'll be doing your children, and society overall, a big favor. Look at the diversity among women we admire: Ellen Degeneres, Sally Ride, Maya Angelou, J. K. Rowling, Rosa Parks, Lily Tomlin, Melissa McCarthy, Duchess Catherine, Agatha Christie, Katharine Hepburn, Oprah, Mother Teresa. There is room for all of us to be who we are.

Teens especially are vulnerable to ridicule, shaming, and bullying in our highly competitive culture, which expects them to sort out a lot of information and develop a lot of maturity in a short amount of time. Don't add to their pain by laying more expectations on them of how a boy or girl "should" act, speak, or dress. Parents have a keen responsibility to protect their children from external forces that would shame them and teach them to quiet the voices of shame from within. We have the power, by loving and accepting our children as they are, to counteract the cruelty they may experience outside of our homes.

FreedHearts Work

Make a list of traits you have considered to be masculine. Do you think that such a list would help or hinder people, especially males but also females? How do you think messages like this have hindered people in your life? What kind of messages about masculinity or femininity have you communicated to your children? How have these messages helped or hindered your children as they've struggled with their sexuality or gender identity?

PART 3

RESPONDING IN LOVE

CHAPTER 15

EMBRACE YOUR CHILD

Your child is not dead, is not dying of cancer, didn't get shot, didn't tell you to get the hell out of their life for no reason. Be on your knees thanking God for that.

—Patricia

Tony Campolo tells the story of a young woman who came to him when he was a Christian college chaplain, distraught that she had been outed as a lesbian, and now she would have to tell her terribly legalistic father. She was sure that he would reject her as his reading of the Bible only condemned "people like me." So she sat there while Tony called her father.

"Your daughter is sitting here with me," Tony began, and he launched into all the wonderful things she was—an outstanding student, the worship team leader, a fine young woman. Her father agreed. Then Tony said, "And in the next thirty seconds, we're going to find out whether *you're* worthy to be called her father."

Undone by Tony's kindness and grace for his daughter, the father collapsed in tears and said, "My daughter is my daughter, she is still a wonderful person, and I want her to know she will always have a place in my heart and in our church."[1]

The call to a parent is to love and embrace their children, to give them a good start, to help them along the path that is right for *them*, not the path the parents think is right. We hold incredible weight in our children's minds and hearts—we were their first heroes. Just as we always wanted our own parents' approval, so do our kids long for ours.

It's hard to overstate the courage it took your child to tell you about their sexual orientation. I mean, who wants to talk to their parents about their sexuality anyway? That alone takes enormous courage, but all the more when they know full well that what they say will challenge your core beliefs.

In this moment, your child needs to know they did the right thing by telling you. Even if your heart has swollen with fear, doubt, anger, grief, disappointment, shame, anguish, or guilt, don't let that keep you from expressing your complete and unconditional love and admiration for your child. The intensity of your emotions will recede over time. Meanwhile, your child needs to know that telling you was the right choice, that you remain a safe place for them, and that you still love them in every way possible. Be extraordinarily kind to yourself and to your child throughout this process, allowing as much time as needed for this new revelation to sink in.

Remember, the most important thing is to love and embrace one another. If you are struggling with embracing your child right now, pray for God to give you *fresh* love for them. Your love and acceptance of your child are about your own heart, not your child's worthiness.

Imagine for a moment that some tragedy suddenly took your child from you. I can tell you that you would give anything, do *anything*, just to have them back—gay or straight.

One day, I was nearly home when a red pickup truck pulled out so suddenly I barely saw it before it crashed into my little car, spinning me around and up onto the curb. Badly shaken, I somehow unbuckled my seatbelt, grabbed my phone, and made it out to the grass where I sat and wept. I pressed my husband's number. "I'm okay, but I've been in a bad accident. I'm not hurt, but the car is crushed."

Rob appeared in minutes with our two oldest teens, and he held me. The policeman told me I would've been killed had I not been buckled in. I wept, thanking God that I was alive, that no one was hurt. My daughter said, "I was just imagining what it would've been to walk up here to see your dead body." My thoughts exactly. We wept again.

Life is ephemeral, beyond our control, easy to snuff out. Put first things first. You have a beautiful child. Do not let this issue overshadow that truth. Ask God whatever you need to, and let God guide you through this maze. But do not let anything diminish the blessed gift your child is and their place in your family. Now is the perfect time to embrace, kiss, encourage, affirm, and love your child.

FreedHearts Work

How did you respond to your child's coming out? Are you satisfied with your response? Imagine that your child loses their community, has nowhere to go, and finds themselves on the street. Imagine losing them forever. How would you feel about that?

Would you like to revise your response to your child? Is there anything you need to say or do to express your endless love for this child God gave you?

CHAPTER 16

WHERE'S THE LOVE?

Why can't you just love me the way I am?
—countless LGBTQ kids

The first time I marched in a Pride Parade was with PFLAG: Parents and Friends of Lesbians and Gays (www.pflag.org). We held signs that read: "We love our gay children!" "Free Mom Hugs," and "God loves YOU!" Throngs of onlookers smiled and cheered as we walked by. I caught the eye of two women, maybe thirty-five years old, clearly moved that I, a mom, would express my support. I wondered what their lives had been like. Did their parents embrace or reject them? Did they have a loving community? I could only speculate. What I *did* know is that we never outgrow our need to love and be loved, and the world is infinitely sweeter when our parents are among those who embrace us.

Shall I tell you the secret of the so-called "Gay Agenda"? It is to be loved and accepted as is, just like anyone else, without having to change or be changed. There, it's out. Vocal activists will tell you that the "Gay Agenda" is to overhaul cultural and ethical norms. I promise you that the goal of the LGBTQ community and its allies is nothing so nefarious. Simple acceptance. Who doesn't want to be accepted for who they are? But all the other stuff about destroying marriage, perverting children, and dismantling life as we know it—those are hateful lies.

Sometimes we find it easier to bolster our beliefs with conspiracy theories and imagined threats than to sit with uncomfortable ideas and re-evaluate what we've long thought of as true. That is even more true when we are convinced those beliefs are clearly stated in the Bible.

Robin (mentioned in chapter 9) was brave enough to dig deeper into Scripture and see if her beliefs about homosexuality were as plainly stated as she had always thought.

After Emily came out to us, I really think I was in shock for a period of time. Once that wore off just a bit, I ranted and raved and cried out to God. I had no idea how to go forward. I finally decided I had to see and read for myself what the Bible had to say about the subject of homosexuality. I was only familiar with the few "clobber passages" so I started with them. And I cried and wondered what it all meant for my eighteen-year-old Christian daughter. Curiously, I found the verses to be very few in number for such an apparently important sin. So I prayed for God to show me something more. And I promised to seek God daily. And then I began to hear it and read it and see it everywhere: LOVE. You are to love her. Well surely it couldn't be that easy, I thought. Don't we need to help her? Fix her? Try to keep her out of hell? For the next week, in random places, I heard and read the story of the prodigal son three or four times. My Bible reading seemed to overflow with verses on love. From the overwhelming number of love verses, as opposed to the clobber passages, I began to see that this was the true gospel. This love that God had for me, for Emily, for all of us. How very emphatically God stressed love above everything else. From then on, when I would feel down or in despair, God would remind again and again, You are to love her. Love has been my saving grace over the past three years and my daily goal. Above all else, I love and allow God to do the rest.

Many parents have expressed the same sentiment: "I prayed, 'What do I do, God?' and I heard, *'Just love.'*"

If you still think your child is in sin, *help your child by pouring on the love.* As 1 Peter 4:8 states, "[L]ove covers a multitude of sins."

FreedHearts Work

Emily's parents sought and clung to the Bible's many *love* verses as they came to peace with Emily's sexuality. In so doing, they transformed their relationship—with God, with each other, and with their beloved Emily. Read through the few below prayerfully, and listen for God's still, small voice. Search your own Bible for more.

> The LORD is merciful and gracious, slow to anger and abounding in steadfast love.
>
> (Ps. 103:8)

> For I am convinced that neither death, nor life, nor angels, nor rulers, nor things present, nor things to come, nor powers, nor height, nor depth, nor anything else in all creation, will be able to separate us from the love of God in Christ Jesus our Lord.
>
> (Rom. 8:38–39)

> Above all, clothe yourselves with love, which binds everything together in perfect harmony.
>
> (Col. 3:14)

CHAPTER 17

DON'T SHAME YOUR CHILD

You are the biggest disappointment of my life, and I never want to see you again.

—Mark's mom

The first time my friend and I talked about shame was long before psychologist Brené Brown's great work on shame, and I hardly even knew what the word meant, but I knew it was something big. We as a culture have only begun to realize how much internalized shame we carry, which then springs easily from our lips to our children. We don't mean to do it, but unless we become consciously aware and take conscious steps to overcome it, shame just leaks out of us.

And it hits its mark.

Mark is 65 years old, and he is still embittered by his mother's malicious words. Mark did not choose to be gay, he did not ask to be gay, and he had no control over being gay. But just the fact of his *being* gay (forget about actions) his mother called *the biggest disappointment of her life.*

How do you recover from such a gutting, acerbic

remark? Where do you go when your mother — or father — rejects you? She had been taught that homosexuality was shameful, and she poured her shame out onto her son.

LGBTQ people are especially subject to shame in our culture, which makes the whole process of discovery and disclosure so torturous. Many pastors and Christian leaders have called homosexuality "a particularly evil lie of Satan." To portray homosexuality as uniquely reprehensible is in itself a particularly evil lie of Satan. To single out homosexuality heaps piles of shame on an already challenging situation.

Expand that circle out and you see that churches shame families as well. Shame is taught in many churches, with the messages that gay people are fallen and "deceitfully wicked." LGBTQ persons learn to forget they bear the image of God, and instead they live in shame that they are displeasing (even disgusting) to God. Just as Mark's mother pushed him away because she couldn't deal with the questions he represented, non-affirming churches shove families away for the same reason. Families that don't fit the mold raise too many questions about God, and it's too unsettling.

The gay kid in youth group represents the cognitive dissonance of these two conflicting understandings. We either have to take the path of least resistance and dismiss him, saying, "He is disgusting . . . and probably something wrong with the family too . . . I want nothing to do with them." Or we have to take the road of courage and say, "But I *know* Mike — he's not disgusting. He's the kid my son grew up with. He's not the result of a debased mind given over to idol worship. *Maybe I misunderstood something about that passage. Maybe I misunderstood something about gay people.*"

Instead of being welcomed, the gay person is pushed back in the closet, and their family is pushed in there too, compounding the shame that is poured out on the child.

A young woman posted this in our secret Facebook group for the LGBTQ community. She wrote:

I am 18. My family and I came down to Gulf Shores for a national soccer tournament and my girlfriend was in the same tournament. My team knows and is very accepting. She and I decided to meet on the beach and hang out on one of our days off, but my mom was disgusted. I have never seen a person so disgusted with their own kid and so embarrassed that people knew she was my girlfriend on the beach. She told me I was making my whole team and their families uncomfortable and that she wanted Kate to leave because people were starting to talk to each other and figuring things out. She was just concerned about how she and her family looked. Not how incredibly happy I was to be sitting on a beach talking with the girl I'm in love with. My mom was honestly disgusted by her . . . and more sadly, by me. She made Kate leave a public beach, and she said the most hurtful things to me I won't repeat. I've never been so embarrassed of my sexuality than when I had to approach my girlfriend in front of people and ask her to leave because my mom thought people were uncomfortable and we were being rude by being in public together.

This poor girl. I grasp the mother's profound shame, given what she has probably been taught about LGBTQ people. But by projecting that shame onto her daughter, she is sacrificing her daughter, causing unfathomable damage, and not helping herself. This mom is concerned about her own comfort and how others will view her, not with her daughter, or she wouldn't treat her like this.

I know what the mom wants: she wants to shame her daughter back into a shell so this "issue" doesn't sully the mom's worldview and her perception of herself as a mother. (She *does* feel ashamed at having "produced" a lesbian daughter.) She doesn't want others to talk about her the way she's talked about people. But to quash someone else—our children—for our own comfort is the height of self-absorption.

Complete acceptance, love, and belonging are necessary for full and authentic living—these are our greatest needs. Shame prohibits acceptance, love, and belonging, because shame says something is fundamentally wrong with us. That's the difference between guilt and shame. Guilt is about something we've done. Shame is about who we are. When we feel something is wrong with us, we don't believe we are worthy of love, so we don't fully experience it even when we are loved. Shame isolates us in self-hatred and self-rejection. Shame is the lie at the very root of our identity. If I do something wrong, I can apologize and make amends. But if I am fundamentally wrong, what hope do I have?

You cannot always ward off disdain from without, but you can provide an oasis of life and belonging within. No matter how shocked you are to learn that your child is gay, your duty as a parent is to love them. Don't shame them, and don't let others shame them either. You may not have sorted out all your thoughts on this issue, but you cannot excuse shaming your child for any reason.

FreedHearts Work

Think about what makes you feel shame. According to Brené Brown, shame is a fear of disconnection or abandonment, and we are all hardwired for connection. The only people who do not feel shame (who are not afraid of disconnection) are sociopaths.[1] How have you felt the threat of disconnection? Think about the ways in which you have shamed your child, even accidentally. How have they felt the threat of disconnection? Do you need to take any action steps toward healing and reconciliation with your child?

CHAPTER 18

WHAT ARE THE CONDITIONS OF YOUR UNCONDITIONAL LOVE?

Parents actually said this to their gay son: "Because of my faith, I cannot accept you." Isn't it because of their faith they should completely accept you?

—Regina

Helen always signed her cards to her daughter, "Agape love." *Agape*—that's a big claim. That's God's love. Huge, boundless, unconditional. God's agape (a-gahp-ay) love has no bounds or hindrances. It reminds us of the apostle Paul's words:

> For I am convinced that neither death, nor life, nor angels, nor rulers, nor things present, nor things to come, nor powers, nor height, nor depth, nor anything else in all creation, will be able to separate us from the love of God in Christ Jesus our Lord.
>
> (Rom. 8:38–39)

This is the love Helen claimed to have for her daughter Linda.

Until Linda's daughter Stacey came out as a lesbian and Linda supported her. Helen badgered Linda, telling her she had no right to "encourage Stacey and those people in this lifestyle."

The expression of love for both daughter and granddaughter stopped. The phone calls stopped. Unconditional love? Agape love? All evaporated. Apparently, Helen's "agape love"—that inexhaustible love of God for us, *no matter what*—turned out to be exhausted. Helen may as well have told Linda, "I love you with God's unconditional love, as long as you meet certain conditions." Love that has requirements is only conditional approval, subject to change.

"Oh, I love Linda *and Stacey*," Helen says still, "but I can't approve of this." Linda is not asking Helen to approve of this—she knows how deeply entrenched her beliefs are. But Linda *is* asking Helen to love her and Stacey unconditionally, to be there for them as her daughter and granddaughter, *regardless of agreement or disagreement*. And for all her talk about "upholding God's standards" and other things Jesus did *not* tell her to do, Helen is saying, "No" to Jesus' directive to love.

What is love anyway? Love means to accept someone exactly as they are and to give room for who they might become. Love does not mean that everything about that person must meet our standards of acceptance—God knows we all shake our heads at our children's behavior and our children may very well shake their heads at ours. That is no reason to reject each other.

I love how Jesus looked over Jerusalem and wept, because he was moved to compassion and he grieved. NOT because they were so derelict and disobedient that he just couldn't stand it. (If that were true he would have been right there behind the religious leaders of his day, encouraging their plan to make everybody more obedient — but he *wasn't.*) No, Jesus wept because "they were like a sheep without a shepherd." They were lost without somebody to tenderly guide them, to scoop them up and hold them. Jesus was there to do that, but they couldn't see it.

God is not grieved because of "all the homosexuals." Not in the very least. That's religious people you're thinking of.

If God is grieved it's because the beautiful, incomparable message of redemption and grace, the sweet peace of a loving relationship, has been truncated, rerouted into a message of behavior-modification and sin-management. For proof, look at Jesus' reaction to the religious leaders who required exactly that kind of sin-management from the people they were supposed to be there to serve. God's incomparable outreach to humanity in the form of Jesus has become "Doing the right thing so you don't get in trouble." Unthinkable.

FreedHearts Work

Have you found the conditions of your unconditional love? Though none of us love as fully as God does, do you see where you might need to break down the walls that limit your love?

CHAPTER 19

SURRENDER CONTROL

I don't know why we say we'd give up our lives for our kids when we won't even give up our point of view. I think we are more selfish than we want to admit.

—Vicky

As far back as I can remember, I have avoided cracks on sidewalks. I don't remember how it started, but it was an unconscious way to seek some measure of control in my uncontrollable world. What I do remember is an unpredictable childhood, distracted and fighting parents, and the death of my mother and three brothers. I later learned that obsessive-compulsive behavior such as avoiding cracks is one of the mind's great coping mechanisms. It is the ability to create meaning in an unpredictable, unstable world.

But OCD behavior is not control at all—it only feels like control. If you want to see this OCD behavior in action, watch athletes' little rituals, such as Tennis Pro Rafael Nadal before each serve. What begins as helpful becomes *unhelpful* once the risk that drove us to that behavior has passed. To avoid sidewalk cracks does not give life to me as a grown woman but withdraws life, in the form of distracted and misspent energy. Remnants of adaptive-behavior-turned-maladaptive behavior *hurt* rather than help, but because we are so used to these things we do, we have a hard time seeing them, much less surrendering them.

Parents (and the rest of us) are full of protective behavior—we seek to reduce risk, to protect ourselves from others' judgment—these are some of the more intractable adaptive-turned-maladaptive behaviors. We don't purposely hurt our children. But we do so unwittingly whenever we ask them to change because of what others will think.

We say we would take a bullet for our kids, and we want to believe it, but a parent is seldom required to take a bullet for their child.

Yet we *are* asked something that, judging by our reaction, is much, much harder. We're asked to take a good cold look at our own beliefs, our own areas of comfort, our own areas of fear. After that good long look, we are asked to abandon maladaptive behavior; we are asked to change our point of view; we are asked to surrender control.

Many of us are used to controlling our world—it makes us feel secure. But you cannot control your way out of this. The more you try to control, the more control will defy you. God has a way of rocking our tiny world by giving us quandaries we don't expect. God shakes everything until all that's left is the unshakable. But parents try so hard to protect their children from the very things that showed them their own need for God.

Yes, parents have life experience. Of course our children would do well to consider the years of wisdom we have to offer. *But their lives are their own.* We do not live inside their hearts and minds. We need to respect our children as individuals, just as we needed our parents to respect us—however foolish we may have been in *our* lives.

Did you take a path your parents disagreed with? Did you make mistakes? And did your unique path show you more than you could've learned by doing what your parents laid out for you? Of course. Life is a journey, not a destination.

The Bible's encouragement to "train up a child in the way they should go" literally means "train them up according to their bent," according to the particular way that God designed them. You must surrender the particulars you have in mind, whatever they are, or you're going to harm your relationship with your child.

I have seen this dynamic many times over in families whose parents hold impossible standards and will not give their kids room to be who they are. I was so disheartened by the impossible position parents put their kids in, especially Christian parents, I wrote a book about it called *How Not to Lose Your Teen.*[1] Haven't you ever made really bad decisions—as a teen or young adult or last month? *So will your kids.* That is part of how we learn and grow. Often parents micromanage their children because they think that will protect them from any possible harm. But harm-free lives were never part of the program. Trust God and grow in your dependence on God. Micromanaging is dependence on *you.*

If parents would simply love and embrace their creative, intelligent, amazing children—including their LGBTQ children—they would see an unfathomable return. They would watch them blossom into the joyful and confident adults they were meant to be. We cannot possibly know the paths our children will take, no matter how clear we think our vision for their futures might be. However, God *does* know our children's paths and is big enough to take care of you, your child, and your whole family. Your job is to love people, especially your child. Let God use this situation to show you what it means to love unconditionally. As we love others, God is at work in ways we can't see.

FreedHearts Work

Do you see the places you're holding onto control over your child's life? It may be large or small ways. (If you're not sure, you can ask your child—as long as you don't get mad at them about the answer.)

Ask God to help you actively surrender control. Say, "God, this child is *yours*." And watch, in due time, how much freedom and love and joy you will experience.

CHAPTER 20

LET GO OF YOUR PLANS

I asked God what to do for my gay son. God answered, "Love what he loves!" That I could do.

—Sara

Even more than teens, adult children are beyond your parental authority. Do not try to direct their choice of spouse, career, or anything else. It just doesn't work. If they ask for your wisdom, give it. But give it with an open hand, with no expectations that they will follow it. You must let them come into their own. Your love and approval should not depend on how they respond; that is conditional love and has no part in a parent-child relationship.

Don't you know someone who longed to play piano but his father pushed him toward football? Do you know a woman whose father got in the way of her and the man she wanted to marry? My beautiful friend, Melinda, remained single her entire life because her father disapproved of every eligible suitor. Aaron gave up his law practice after ten years because he realized he never wanted it in the first place; it had been Dad's idea. As in movies like *Dead Poets Society* and *The Notebook*, this parent-controlled path doesn't end well.

One of my readers, Scott, wrote this on my blog:

When I came out to my parents, I discovered which parent loved me unconditionally and it wasn't the one I expected. My rather stoic Dad simply looked at me and said, "You're my son, and that's that." My mother, on the other hand, fussed for years over everything from "What will the neighbors think?" to "I won't have any grandchildren" (even though my brother was straight) to "It's just wrong." My Dad was the one who finally had to tell her to stop it because, in his words, "If you make Scott choose between you and Dennis, he'll choose, and you won't like the choice he makes—you will never see him again."

I understand the fear that pushes Mom around on this, but that is between her and God. It is not Scott's job to hide who he is so Mom will feel better. It's Mom's job to seek greater understanding and peace and love for her son (and his partner).

You have done your best as a parent, however flawed you were. Weren't we all? Time to trust God with this child you raised. Do not shun them or take action against them, which will only alienate you from their lives. Look around at kids whose parents have shown unconditional love, and see their beautiful relationship. Then look at those whose parents stood in judgment of their children and see how that's worked out for them. Instead of manipulating your adult child by withholding approval based on their behavior, it's time to let them go.

You have many major life events ahead. Those events won't look the way you pictured them, but neither does most of life. Graduations, first loves, true loves will still happen— will you be a part of it? You still may have weddings and grandchildren. *And you may not. You may not have even if your child was straight.* Remember that those dreams—however

normal to hope for, however entitled you feel to have them —
are still *your* dreams. They may not be what God has in mind
for them, nor what they have in mind for themselves. Best
to let them go and welcome the life that is ahead. You may
discover reality more beautiful than you could possibly have
imagined. Whatever is ahead, you want to be part of it and
your child wants you to be part of it. Be there for them as
you wanted your parents to be there for you.

This road is likely not one you would have chosen nor
initially welcomed. But if you seek, God will show you the
beauty of the journey. Perhaps *you* were chosen to shine
God's love amidst all the anger and hate (even if your
beliefs about it never change). Perhaps God will work
through you to help restore God's name, which has been
so maligned to a large community of people who need to
know God loves them (as we *all* do).

Every person's deep hope and even need is to hear their
father's and mother's sincere, "I love you, my child; I'm
proud of you." No, ifs, ands, or buts — just unconditional
acceptance. *And our job as parents is to grant that unconditional
love to our children.* Before anyone gets high and mighty
about how disappointing their child is to them, listing all
the reasons said child has fallen short, remember that you
also have your issues, and someone could make a similar
list about you. Our job is to love, pure and simple. The
classic little book *The Blessing* talks about the importance
of giving our blessing to our children. We need to give it,
and they need to receive it. Don't waste another minute to
bless your child, love your child, and set your child free.

FreedHearts Work

Talk about the ways in which you have held on to specific
plans for your child. How do you need to let those go?

(I'm not saying they will not happen, just that you have to let them go to happen or not.) In what areas are you withholding approval from your child? Think about all the ways in which you might set your child free by letting go of the reins of their life. If you're not sure, ask God for a visual. Then take the hard step of letting it go.

CHAPTER 21

BEAR THEIR BURDENS

Craig and his father had this conversation:
"Son, just try to date girls."
"Dad, I have."
"What about your girlfriend, Heather?"
"Yeah, that was me trying."
"I think you're selfish for not trying harder to find another girl
you like."
"No, Dad, it's selfish to continue to date girls when I'm gay. I'm
not bringing another girl into this."

Think about the mountains your child had to move to authentically be who they are. They risked everything: approval of family, friends, and community. They had to put it *all* on the line with no guarantee it would ever work out. When have you had to do that?

Yet, they were courageous enough to do it.

On the other hand, parents—and community—can be incredibly selfish when it comes to their gay kids. They want what they want so much, they can't see any other perspective. Nick wrote me that his family disowned him, did not speak to him for thirty years. Then when his father lay dying, his brother called Nick to come care for him.

None of the other siblings would do it, but Nick, hoping for restored relationship, went to his father's bedside.

This is a surprisingly common story, believe it or not; I have heard it several times. A gay child is excluded until the end when the family needs them. I can't even wrap my head around doing that to another person.

Imagine looking at your son after lost decades, years you could never restore. And many of these stories still don't end in a nice reconciliation for all. That is the excluded one's hope, but many times the family is just using someone to do the "dirty work" and then excluding them once more.

Having a gay child brings a lot of tough questions. It cracks our paradigm. It draws looks from neighbors. Don't shift all that to your child but instead *help lift* that burden. Let the weight of the discomfort rest on you. Your child is carrying enough weight as it is. They already fear disappointing others. They probably feel pressure to change their identity, protect their family, and fight their own doubts about God's acceptance. Don't press for answers or easy solutions. As with other big events in life, get comfortable with not knowing how it will all work out, and patiently let God reveal the answers in the right timing.

My friend was shocked when her sixteen-year-old revealed she was pregnant. Hard news, of course. It affected her schooling and her future. Friends had plenty to say—they always do. But that mom helped her daughter.

Isn't that the least we can do for our own children? Harsh parents may say, "You brought this on yourself—you take care of it," but that is not a kind or loving response. Surely we can imagine being in that position, had the tables been turned.

Your child coming out to you no doubt stirs up many questions, doubts, and fears. If possible, find other help, *real* help, for yourself. Work it through with a trusted friend, counselor, affirming pastor, or other trusted ally. For your well-being and your child's, do *not* listen to people who say this is terribly wrong and that you must confront your child. What you *don't* need right now is others' uninformed opinions. You need real empathy and support. You need truly affirming friends.

Defend your child from others or insist that others keep their opinions to themselves. Resist turning on your child for "bringing this on the family." Believe me, your child *already knows* people disapprove. They also know people want them to change and usually, if they could, they would. You need to stand up for your child and *be there for them.*

Talk with your child as much as they want, but not more. As they navigate the rest of their world, be their safe haven. Paul told his mother, "I had to wait to tell you until I knew that I would be okay if you guys rejected me." That broke her heart, because she never would have rejected him in a million years. But his point is well taken; he has seen plenty of friends rejected by their families after coming out. By staying true to your child, by embracing and loving them, you can assure them that even if the world shuts them out, they still have you. Your relationship with your child calls for that much.

Once your child has come out, you may be heartbroken for all the time they walked this journey alone, but be at peace. Trust that you learned of it at just the right time. As one thirty-five-year-old gay man said, "That was a journey I had to take myself; my parents could not have shared that with me."

Jesus calls us to love each other, encourage each other, and bear with one another. You are uniquely positioned to help bear your child's burden and so fulfill the law of Christ (Gal. 6:2). Jesus never tells us to fix everything — that's *God's* job!

FreedHearts Work

How have you borne your child's burdens over the years? Maybe you drove them to and from countless sports or dance practices simply because they wanted to participate—or maybe you spoke up when they were bullied at school. Reflect on that. How might you need to bear your child's burdens when it comes to living fully in their orientation or identity? Remember that if your child is still breathing, it's never too late to express your love.

PART 4

WORKING IT OUT
WITH GOD

CHAPTER 22

DON'T DESTROY
YOUR CHILD'S FAITH

My Christianity had died the death of a thousand nicks and cuts.
—Bart Campolo

I'm convinced that it is not the hard things our faith requires of us, some crosses we are unwilling to bear, that destroys our faith. It is the "thousand nicks and cuts" that hack away at us, day after day—the shaming from family, the disdain in our own church, the requirements of the leadership or the youth leader—that make our kids (or us) finally say, "I'm done." Though the bridge may fall down in one piece, its supports have been eroding for years.

Bart Campolo, son of renowned evangelical leader Tony Campolo, speaks for a generation for whom Christianity has been tied to so many extraneous pieces, it will no longer bear the weight, so it all comes crashing down. Our LGBTQ kids face a thousand shaming and destabilizing events—which we never see—that undermine them and their faith. Picture Indiana Jones with his leather pants and boots, hacking away through thorn vines with a machete; he's going to be fine. Picture his companion Marion traversing the same path with her dress torn off short and her high heels in her hand—*she has a completely different experience.* Her bare legs and feet will sustain more nicks and cuts than Indy will, and he's oblivious. It is Indy's job (with his superior gear) to protect Marion, and it is our job (with our privileged status as straight, grown-up, financially independent adults) to protect our children.

Our children face a thousand nicks and cuts to which we are likewise oblivious. We're not necessarily negligent, but those homophobic remarks don't cut and bruise us the same way. And that steady stream of shame and hate have eroded the foundations of our kids' true faith.

You may still have many doubts and questions about your child's sexuality. *Is it a sin? Did God really make my child this way? Am I a bad Christian if I condone homosexuality?* It's okay to keep wrestling with these things. But do your wrestling with God, not with your child. Show your child the unconditional love of Christ, and work out any reservations you still have with God. The following chapters will help you in that process.

When children who have been clobbered by Christians' hurtful words and actions still *have* faith, it's because God preserved it in spite of the toxicity. Many parents who've come around are worried about their children's faith. I encourage them to let go and love them. Let them breathe and stretch into the love they've needed. Let God handle their faith. If you are concerned about your child's faith, *let go* the requirements and let God be God. People look at the outward appearance, but God looks at the heart. If we insist on correcting the outward appearance, we will destroy our child's heart.

Your child's faith is a precious thing. Don't let it be destroyed. There's a joke that in seminary they take your faith away at the beginning and return it to you at the end.

One student voiced that to Lewis Donelson, our beloved and knowledgeable New Testament professor at Austin Presbyterian Theological Seminary. Lewis answered kindly, "I would never try to take your faith away. Faith is a tender thing that should be nurtured. Blow on those embers and keep them going. And how could we ever give your faith back to you at the end? How would we know how to preserve it, and how could we give it back without damaging it? On the contrary, faith is something to treasure and protect."

His words brought tears to my eyes. Of *course* we need to nurture our faith—it is our sacred treasure. Faith is a precious relationship with God, planted by deeply personal interactions directly with God, fed and watered by hope and joy. Faith is our birthright as human beings created in God's image.

Our beliefs are a different matter. Our beliefs, our rigidly held interpretations, become our prejudice, our harshness, our judgment. Every generation has had to face and dismantle false beliefs about the universe (that the earth is flat), about people (that women are "deformed males"), and about God (that God is all about rules, which Jesus handily dismantles).

In seminary, I've had to pull out some of my *beliefs*, lay them in pieces on the table, and scrutinize them. My *faith*, on the other hand, has been kindled and inspired. I have more trust in God now than I've ever had—it just looks a lot less like the tenets of the church where I first found it.

Now here's the part that really breaks my heart: many tenderhearted LGBTQ souls have been stripped of their faith by people unwilling to examine their own beliefs. Adolescents who pour their hearts out to God to make sense of who they are, only to be told their faith is wrong and their beliefs will send them to hell. Aging gay men who have long since come to terms with who they are, yet are still haunted by horrific words of their parents or pastors. People being told that childlike faith is not enough, they also have to keep impossible rules. This is blasphemy spoken by religious detractors who are unwilling to surrender their control and let God be God.

No, no, and no. In the words of my wise professor, "Faith is fragile, we need to protect it." No one has the right to rip it away. Think about how kind Jesus is, always kind, to the down and out. He does not chide them for their lack of faith but encourages the faith they have. And he defends them from the religious ones imposing standards. To follow Christ is likewise to be kind to those who are struggling and to defend them against the religious ones imposing standards.

Jesus had the harshest words for those who would rip away someone's faith. "If any of you put a stumbling block [literally, "set a trap for them"] before one of these little ones who believe in me, it would be better for you if a great millstone were fastened around your neck and you were drowned in the depth of the sea" (Matt. 18:6).

Don't let that be you.

FreedHearts Work

Where has your faith faltered over the years? What has lifted you back up again? What do you believe today that you didn't believe five years ago? Can you see how you have grown in your faith? Can you take anything from that into your experience today?

Where have you seen your child struggle in their faith? Many parents tell me their child wants nothing to do with God—they may call themselves atheists. (Who can blame them, given what they have been told about God?) Are you willing to let that be what it is, leave their faith in

God's hands, and simply love them? I know that this can be excruciating. But if you are able to shift your focus from their faith and just focus on loving them and loving God, in a few years, you will be amazed by what you see!

CHAPTER 23

YOU DON'T HAVE
TO PROTECT GOD

*You have enough time for what God wants you to do. You do not
have enough time for what God's people want you to do.*
— Dwight Edwards

My young Hannah once came to me with a nightmare,
but she wouldn't tell me about it, because she said
it would scare me. Finally, *finally,* she told me: she had
dreamed that someone had grabbed me and stolen my
watch. (She was talking about my favorite watch I'd got-
ten in Italy years before.) To her childish mind, this was a
disaster, but I was touched that she'd tried to protect me so
I wouldn't be afraid. How sweet is that? The thing about
being her mother, though, is that it's my job to protect *her,*
not hers to protect *me.*

Many Christians have their faith upside down. They
want to protect God from sin. This "nightmarish LGBTQ
situation" terrifies them in the culture, in the church, and
God forbid it should get in their homes. They are sure God
can't handle it. They *must* stamp it out.

We need to reverse that flow. *Let God comfort us.* Isn't

God much better positioned to comfort us than we are to comfort God? Then we can comfort *others* with that same comfort God has given us.

> Blessed be the God and Father of our Lord Jesus Christ, the Father of mercies and the God of all consolation, who consoles us in all our affliction, so that we may be able to console those who are in any affliction with the consolation with which we ourselves are consoled by God. For just as the sufferings of Christ are abundant for us, so also our consolation is abundant through Christ.
>
> (2 Cor. 1:3–5)

That's what all those verses mean: bear each other's burdens, encourage each other, lift each other up. You see how it fits together? God comforts us because we are the children in that relationship, we comfort each other, as siblings, and we comfort our own children. What a beautiful plan.

When we focus on sin, we live in fear. When we "protect" God or hide our true questions and concerns from God, we sacrifice the comfort God would give us, and then we have nothing to give each other.

The sewage stream of fear should flow through the plumbing and out of the house toward God, who's well able to handle it. When we don't let God be God, we've reversed the flow, and the septic fear has backed up onto the floor and is knee-deep on the carpet. Now we scurry around in a panic micromanaging each other and searching for a plunger. We have no joy, no peace, no love.

Take your fears, your questions, your anger, your grief and lay them at God's feet. God knows what you're feeling anyway. Pour out your heart, scream at the heavens, wrestle with God, and let God comfort you.

In fact, the reward at the end of this rainbow-colored

journey may indeed result in a much deeper relationship with God, a deeper ability to love and show compassion to others and to receive love and grace, and a heart that is free to love and be loved by God and others. If you just stay on the path of faith and follow where God leads your heart, you will find the peace that passes understanding.

FreedHearts Work

Think about the ways in which your faith has changed through all this. Has it made you more fearful? Can you see how God may be pulling down old God-paradigms? Even if that freedom scares you to pieces, does it also appeal to you, even thrill you? Imagine what closeness you and God can experience.

CHAPTER 24

GOD'S GOT THIS

I knew it would work out because — spoiler alert — it always works out!

—Sabrina

In the 1986 movie *Labyrinth*, as Sarah (Jennifer Connelly) tries to make her way through the labyrinth, she comes to a wall. Worm tells her to walk through it, but she points out that there's no way through it — *it's a wall.* Worm laughs. "Course there is! You try walking through it; you'll see what I mean!" Sarah can't get her head around walking through the wall, but Worm says, "Things are not always what they seem in this place. So, you can't take anything for granted." To her surprise, Sarah walks through the wall.

People talk about God — the God of the universe — in absolute terms, in black-and-white terms, as if we know where the wall opens and where it doesn't, as if the Bible reveals everything there is to know about God. We read about slaying giants with a stone and facing lions in a den, but we live as though God is stagnant and quite small.

We claim to trust God, but we have far too small a box for God to live in.

Christians are fond of saying that God does not change. But cultures do change, and we often find that our moral thinking has been shaped more by culture than we realize. For example, lefties used to be considered backward, maladjusted, or even evil—with inadequate mothers. That is no longer the cultural thinking. Interracial marriage used to be considered against God's natural design. The majority of our culture no longer believes that. Society is rapidly changing its views on homosexuality and marriage equality. Marriage equality is now the law of the land, hand in hand with acceptance.

Individuals in a culture change over time as well. We change and grow and learn, and our lives change as we do. Life is a meandering river, not a straight path. Let your child grow without trying to get them to grow in a certain direction. Did you anticipate at eighteen where you are right now? At eighteen, I did not think I would marry, and I definitely thought I would not have children. I'm not sure how twenty-eight years with Rob and five children happened, but there it is.

If your child has expressed doubts or confusion about their sexuality, don't panic. For teens, many changes are still to come. Let them discover their own life path. Change is an expected part of life. What did you know at eighteen that you feel the same about today? Come to think of it, sexual orientation may be one of the few things you *were* sure about. At this time of your child's life, the sky is the limit. Give them room to spread their wings and fly their own arc. Do not require a certain path. Haven't we yet learned how crippling it is to have to please someone else? One friend confided how disheartened her son feels because his dad will not accept him as he is:

Caleb will not discuss this with his dad, and the discussions Mel and I have had have been pretty discouraging.

Caleb is now pushing the envelope in other ways because of it. I worry about how this lack of acceptance is eroding his strong Christian faith with this sexual identity he is discovering.

Instead of clipping their wings, be the wind beneath them. God is big enough to handle them without your rejection to prove your point. Trust God to guide your child as needed while you love unconditionally.

My friends Linda and Rob Robertson lost their son to drugs after taking the path of "reorientation" endorsed by the church.[1] "We taught him to hate his sexuality," Linda said years later. When asked if she would have gone to her son's wedding, she said, "Of course. I'd much rather go to my gay child's wedding than his funeral."

Consider that *straight* was not God's plan for your child—if it were, your child would *be* straight. Have faith that God has got your child, even if your child hasn't got God. Is your child strong enough to push God away? Have faith that the more freedom you give your child, the more they will come to the best place for them, sooner or later. Have faith that to find the right path for one's life takes time, and it usually includes many false starts. Please, give your child that freedom.

Micah 6:8 sums up our role beautifully: "He has told you, O mortal, what is good; and what does the LORD require of you but to do justice, and to love kindness, and to walk humbly with your God?"

FreedHearts Work

Extraordinary circumstances are often the best cutter to open the box we put God in. How have you kept God in a box on this issue? How have you kept your child in a box on this issue? Where do you feel the Spirit pulling you to be the wind beneath your child's wings? How could you love, encourage, and free your child from your family's expectations and from their fear of disappointing people?

CHAPTER 25

THE ULTIMATE FEAR: HELL

I have moments of complete peace where I can share pictures and experiences, but then I have moments of absolute fear and sadness about what's happening. All the ugliness from my church has devastated me, and I guess I'm grieving—but I am NOT afraid my daughter is going to hell because of who she is.

*—*Peggy

We were at a FreedHearts Moms gathering, joined by Stan Mitchell, pastor of GracePointe Church in Franklin, Tennessee. One mom said it was hard for her to believe in a literal, eternal hell where her son would burn because he was gay. Stan answered her:

> We don't really believe it. I sat at my Uncle Tim's funeral at eleven years old, and I began to know something was up. Uncle Tim was a good man, he lived a better Christian life than most of us, but he didn't go to church because he'd figured that preacher out a long time ago. But we knew that "Tim was going to hell because he didn't go to church like we did and it was such a tragedy." We always tried to get him to go to church. We put in prayer requests: "Pray for Tim because he's going to

hell." And then when Uncle Tim died, we all cried at the funeral, because Uncle Tim was going to hell. And 30 minutes later we were back at the church fellowship hall eating potato salad and banana pudding like there was no tomorrow. They were laughing and telling jokes. And I'm looking at them like, "What are you doing? Uncle Tim's burning! And you're eating potato salad?" And something inside of me said, "Either these are the meanest sons of bitches that ever lived, or we don't believe that."

Hell is a horrific fear. We human beings toss the word *hell* around as if it's something we can even comprehend. Stan's story reveals that belief in a literal burning hell is problematic. How can we believe in hell and still trust God? That doubt does not keep Christians from using hell to scare people, though. If we insist on the existence of hell, we must reassess Jesus' character witness of God because, for sure, Jesus' description of a loving God whom we can approach boldly and a God who sends real people to a literal burning hell do not fit together, no matter how much mental gymnastics we employ.

I do not seek to uproot your theology; I seek to give you permission to follow your heart where the Spirit leads. If you doubt the existence of hell, you are not alone, even among stalwart and Bible-believing Christians. I offer this alternative view so that you don't have to live in torment over the idea of eternal damnation. Some Christians are afraid to be lax about hell and then find it exists. But we must consider the exorbitant cost of living this life in fear of hell if it does *not* exist. If you are being perfectly honest, you must admit that Jesus was pretty nonchalant about—and said precious little about—something that, if true, would be the biggest threat conceivable. What he did say referred to the dump called Gehenna, which burned outside the city day and night. Gehenna, or Gei Hinnom, and Sheol, the Hebrew word for the land of the dead, have all been conflated and all translated to English indiscriminately as *hell*.[1] As Benjamin L. Corey points out in his blog on Patheos, the word "hell" that we use today, doesn't actually appear in language until long after the first century, in roughly 725 CE.[2]

But despite the concept's dubious origins, it scares us just to *question* hell's existence. We can hardly even question whether homosexuality is wrong, as it has been strangely and singularly tied to hell. Why should it scare us to *ask the question?* Because we immediately think: "If I'm wrong about this, what else am I wrong about?" Suddenly the ground under you shakes and you feel as if you can't trust anything you thought you knew. This is a significant problem. I believe that is why the church took two centuries to accept a heliocentric solar system. "If we're wrong about this, what else are we wrong about?" We recoil. We withdraw the question. We *really* want to feel safe.

But what if we did this instead: what if we pressed into God—the God we say we trust—and let a new understanding emerge?

If you are shaking right now, or ready to throw this book in the toilet, step back for a moment. We're just asking questions here, and God never punished anyone for asking questions. Instead, let me encourage you in this: even if you staunchly believe in hell, the Bible does *not* say *anyone* will go to hell for being LGBTQ. It's just not in there. Be at peace, and rest. And let God reveal to you whatever you need to know.

FreedHearts Work

What are your biggest fears for your child, for yourself, for your faith? Can you lay them on the table and look at them anew? Seek the Spirit of God in you for understanding? If hell is of concern to you, are you willing to seek God about it and listen for the Spirit stirring in your heart?

CHAPTER 26

THE SLIPPERY SLOPE
OF SIN

"The challenge of all challenges is to think of detouring from what we've been taught all our lives—how scary is that?! But not to embrace them is much more destructive to the gospel than to love and fully accept them."

—John

You may have been frightened into believing the "slippery slope" argument that if we "accept homosexuality," it's a straight decline to accepting all kinds of god-awful things. That's how it's posed, followed up with terribly offensive comparisons to incest and bestiality. The slippery slope argument is based on the idea that our job is to decide which sins are unacceptable and then reject them, to somehow hold the line on those sins for others. The idea is to stay perched precariously at the top of some imaginary hill, where one false move will plunge us right into the sewage. Where is the deep peace Paul speaks of in Philippians 4:7? Or the light burden Jesus promises in Matthew 11:30? This argument is meant to intimidate, and it does a good job of it.

Once you buy into that premise, then you find yourself on your own slippery slope to judgment, harshness, cruelty. You end up excluding and dis-fellowshipping and ostracizing, based on your best view of the situation. Is that really the Spirit of God?

Come over here with me to look at this thing from a completely different angle. Let's consider the fact that *Jesus never gave us that job*. Jesus told us repeatedly not to judge another's (God's) servant, to treat others as we would want to be treated.

Let's consider that Jesus in fact *encourages* the slippery slope. He accepts the lowest of the low. He embraces the very ones the religious elite reject. He goes from bad to worse as he breaks down every barrier those religious leaders put up to keep out "sinners." He scandalously lets a "sinful woman" wash his feet with her voluptuously unfastened hair. He daringly eats dinner in the house of a tax extortionist. Out of control, he breaks the Sabbath laws by *healing*, of all things.

Whoa, Jesus, what is going on?

Then Jesus takes that slippery slope plunge all the way down to the bottom, as he describes God in unthinkable terms—as a father lifting his skirts to *run* to embrace his errant son, as a man who throws a wedding feast that nobody attends, as a (gasp) *woman* who searches high and low for her lost coin. Then, worst of all, *Jesus compares himself to God*.

Two thousand years later, as though they have never read these stories, the same religious leaders are intimidating Christians who accept people freely the way Jesus did. We should not be afraid of accepting too freely but rather afraid of *rejecting* others too easily. The real slippery slope is judgment, defining sin, increasing hate: all those things Jesus warned us about.

You may now be thinking, "But we have to define sin. We have to make judgments. There has to be some line drawn."

If so, let's recall Jesus' words: "Do not judge, so that you may not be judged. *For with the judgment you make you will be judged,* and the measure you give will be the measure you get" (Matt. 7:1–2; emphasis added). When you do judge, use the kindest standards possible. That is how we would want to be judged, right? The place to get harsh is where Jesus got harsh, when people are using the threat of God to hurt other people.

It's true that accepting others is a slippery slope. But it's *not* a treacherous slip into the sewer. No. It is instead an exhilarating bobsled ride out onto the level ground where *all* are welcome, where *all* are in the family. The real slippery slope—that Jesus is on and invites *us* on—is the slide into inclusion of *all* God's family, because all are created in God's image. We need not get bent out of shape about other people's growth; any growth we need comes from God anyway.

Jesus, the original proponent of the slippery slope, invites true followers to love and include those the religious leaders rejected, and he blasts the religious leaders for rejecting *anyone*. What is the greatest command? *Love.* Love God, love your neighbor. Who is your neighbor? Everyone. That's all we need to know.

Once you stop looking for who you can *exclude*, you begin to look for who you will *include*. The slippery slope of loving inclusion will lead to an avalanche of mercy and justice and love—the very things Jesus told us to be about: "Go and learn what this means, 'I desire mercy, not sacrifice.' For I have come to call not the righteous but sinners" (Matt. 9:13).

FreedHearts Work

Think about times you have held back from wholeheartedly embracing someone—family, friend, or neighbor—because you disagreed with something in that person's life. Did you succeed in changing that aspect of the friend or neighbor's life? Did that make you happy? Or did the relationship fracture? Where did Jesus tell you to withhold love based on where you think others are wrong? If you cannot answer that last question, it's time to let go and be the loving and embracing person you were called to be.

CHAPTER 27

THE "CLOBBER PASSAGES" (OLD TESTAMENT)

If the you of five years ago doesn't consider the you of today a heretic, you are not growing spiritually.

—Thomas Merton

Have you ever asked yourself why, out of 31,000 verses in the Bible, some Christians uproot six verses from any context and then clobber LGBTQ people and allies with them? What is that all about? These people trample over numerous other passages (about not judging, letting the Holy Spirit guide, loving unconditionally) to drop down these few mistranslated, poorly exegeted, and disproportionately represented verses as if they are God's final word. Like a teen clamoring over piles of trash and dishes and clothes piled in her room to triumphantly point out *your* lunch dishes still stacked on the dining room table. You wonder if maybe this teen, like those verse-wielders, has a bigger point to prove than "truth."

That is the case with those who are obsessed with these few passages, pulled out of context, to prove a point. If you have had these verses thrown out at you or your child, or if you yourself are stuck on the seeming condemnation of these verses, let's take a closer look and pray that God will help put those concerns to rest that have inflamed in your heart.

People often say "The Bible is very clear about this," when in fact, about most things, the Bible is *not* clear at all. This phrase is a catchall, so the person saying it doesn't really have to answer for their interpretation. But what they're saying is "clear" *is*, in fact, an interpretation. For any particular text, there are more readings than we realize. Whatever particular reading we may have learned in church is usually far from the only one.

For example, in *The JPS Bible Commentary: Esther*,[1] Adele Berlin makes a convincing argument that the book of Esther was written as a farce, full of exaggeration for comedic and political effect. One of the "jokes" she finds in the text includes the measurement for the gallows Haman built: fifty cubits (seventy-five feet) high, as tall as a seven-story building.[2] "Imagine such a structure standing in Haman's backyard!" Berlin writes. "The height of fifty cubits is clearly an exaggeration. No structure that the Bible describes is fifty cubits high. Even Solomon's Temple is only thirty cubits high."

I have read, studied, and been taught the book of Esther in my many years as a Christian, by knowledgeable Bible study teachers and pastors, and I had never heard even the *possibility* that Esther was written as a comedy. Not once. I was likewise surprised to learn that to agree on only one possible reading of any text is a recent development. In the Jewish tradition, with the original scrolls in front of them, rabbis would pontificate on their various interpretations — *and that was all part of the fun.* They were not looking for the correct read but were engaging in community, with God and with each other. Our obsession to seek out the correct read today is to our detriment — it sets us up to judge others, it sacrifices loving community, and it defies trust in God to guide us.

With this same desire to explore interpretations other than what we've long been taught, let's consider the six "clobber passages" used to condemn LGBTQ persons.

Genesis 1:27

> So God created humankind in [God's] image, in the image of God, [God] created them; male and female [God] created them.

This male-female creation is a great picture, but it is not the complete picture. As we discussed in chapter 12, God also created people who are both male and female, and those who are neither male nor female. These people are proof positive that God's ways are bigger than our ways. Christians love to say, "God didn't make a mistake." That's exactly right. So let intersex people stand as God's warning to us not to categorize too swiftly or surely, but humbly default to love (as instructed), and let God hold onto the mysteries.

Genesis 18:16–19:29

Here's the story: two strangers come to Sodom and are going to sleep in the city square, but because the town is so dangerous, Lot pleads with them to come inside his house for safety. Then "the men of Sodom, both young and old" (19:4) come to rape these strangers, but Lot won't let them in. (He does offer them his daughters to rape instead—is this *really* the story we want to refer to for God's moral instruction?) What does this have to do with homosexuality (a word that, by the way, was not even invented until 1870[3] and not used in a version of the Bible until 1946[4])? *No* city's entire male population is gay. It is *not* about being gay; it is about bringing strangers into submission and showing them that they are not welcome.

Ezekiel 16:49 and Jude 7 reference the sinfulness of Sodom, revealing what a mythic status the city had. Jude says the city's notorious depravity included *"sexual immorality"* and *"unnatural lust,"* and by the Middle Ages, "sodomy" had become a synonym for homosexual behavior. Ezekiel, however, was written much closer to the time of Genesis and says nothing about sex. Instead it identifies quite a different problem: the city's attitude toward those in need. "This was the guilt of your sister Sodom: she and her daughters had pride, excess of food, and prosperous ease, but did not aid the poor and needy."

Leviticus 18:22 and 20:13

> You shall not lie with a male as with a woman; it is an abomination.
>
> If a man lies with a man as with a woman, both of them have committed an abomination; they shall be put to death; their blood is upon them.

Okay, let's just slow down a wee bit here. The key is in *"as with a woman."* In the ancient cultural view, for a man to submit himself to the female role, *"as with a woman,"* was to surrender his power and become a woman, or *"deformed man."* Surely we see the patriarchal structure of the ancient world. If we don't, then we're stuck arguing that if our houseguest is threatened, the Bible instructs us to offer our daughter to the assailant instead (Gen. 19:8, above). No one would support such a "theology." Be very careful to keep these verses in their ancient context, lest we end up with crazy beliefs *and actions*.

All that said, even if you disagree that these have been wrongly interpreted, we must still remember that we have been redeemed from the law, and anyone who attempts to live by it is cursed (Gal. 3:10). We excuse hundreds of other Old Testament commands as contextual; not to see these the same way is a *choice*.

FreedHearts Work

How do you tend to view the Old Testament? Think about how you separate what is inspiring and applicable in your life and what is purely reflective of the ancient world in which and for which it was written. Do you treat the passages discussed above differently from other Old Testament admonitions? How do you think you might need to look at these verses now?

CHAPTER 28

THE "CLOBBER PASSAGES" (NEW TESTAMENT)

Being gay is natural. Hating gay is a lifestyle choice.

—John Fugelsang

You may have seen the sign: "This is what Jesus said about homosexuality: . . ." and the rest of the sign is blank. Jesus, the picture of God, had no admonitions whatsoever about homosexuality. For those interested in living a life in the love of Christ, for *Christians* who claim the name of Christ, this is important to know.

These remaining "clobber passages" are from the New Testament. Remarkably, none of these passages are from the Gospels; none of them are from Jesus.

Romans 1:22–32

> For this reason God gave them up to degrading passions. Their women exchanged natural intercourse for unnatural, and in the same way also the men, giving up natural intercourse with women, were consumed with passion for one another. Men committed shameless acts with men and

received in their own persons the due penalty for their error.

(vv. 26–27)

This sounds completely condemning; it was the last clobber verse I understood. As always, though, context is key. Back up a few verses and you see that Paul was referring to those who rejected God to participate instead in idol worship, which included temple sex and other practices we do not even know about today.

But here's the much bigger piece: Paul is using a vice list, a "laundry list" of problems to get us all onboard in agreement that these things are terrible. Verses 29–30 are full of other sins ranging from murder and malice to gossip and rebellion against parents. Then he drops the boom in Romans 2:1 with: "Therefore you have no excuse, whoever you are, when you judge others; for in passing judgment on another you condemn yourself, because you, the judge, are doing the very same things." To use the Romans 1 verse to condemn is to put yourself in the Romans 2 group who condemn themselves. How in trouble we are when we insist on judging.

1 Corinthians 6:9–10 and 1 Timothy 1:10–11

> Do you not know that wrongdoers will not inherit the kingdom of God? Do not be deceived! Fornicators, idolaters, adulterers, male prostitutes, sodomites, thieves, the greedy, drunkards, revilers, robbers—none of these will inherit the kingdom of God.
>
> . . . fornicators, sodomites, slave traders, liars, perjurers, and whatever else is contrary to the sound teaching that conforms to the glorious gospel of the blessed God, which he entrusted to me.

Again, we have the vice lists, designed to tell us *all* to stand down, don't judge, and let God be God. When faced with such lists, our lesser selves tend to pick out a couple of words to bend out of shape and to ignore the other admonitions to "liars" and "promise breakers." Both of these verses use the Greek words *malakoi*[1] (literally "soft" as in "effeminate") and *arsenokoitai*[2] (literally "abusers of themselves with mankind") and translate them as *homosexual, male prostitute, fornicator,* or *sodomite.* Those words are interpretations; the original words did not say this. That is plenty to make a fair-minded person pause and say, "Hmm . . . that's not what it says." It is more than enough to make us stand down and say, "Okay, let's take another look at the context." And that's what many fair-minded pastors and theologians have done, seeking to understand more of what those words might have meant.

That concludes our list of the six verses (or seven, if you include Jude's take on Sodom's sin) that are commonly interpreted to refer to homosexuality, mostly in ways that don't hold up to scrutiny. By comparison, the Bible has some 110 verses about slavery, including direct support of slavery and instructions on how to deal with slaves. Yet, as a culture, we have somehow managed to move on past those verses and *condemn* slavery as against the heart of God. How? We have looked at the overarching heart of God as revealed in Jesus Christ, and we have concluded that slavery is inhumane and inexcusable. To hold onto these few passages to condemn homosexuality reveals the heart of the holdout, *not* the heart of God.

FreedHearts Works

Look to see if any verses remain stuck in your craw. Reread those parts above carefully. Ask God for clarity. Listen to the thoughts that follow. If those thoughts are about love, then congratulations, because you have just realigned with the primary mission of Christ. Join the throngs of parents who received that same message and find your peace there.

If those thoughts are not about love, press into God for deeper understanding.

CHAPTER 29

PLEASE, NO CHILD SACRIFICE

So you're choosing your daughter over God? HELL, YES!
—Arianna

How many times have parents who embrace their children been asked if they are choosing their child over God? It's a crazy legalistic question. Of course it assumes that *God* wants you to inspect/correct/reject your child to the satisfaction of the person asking you this inane question. But you are not choosing your child over God. *You are choosing your child over people who claim to speak for God.*

I am horrified by the child sacrifice in the Old Testament. *Horrified.* Any sane person would be. But apparently some Israelites were drawn into the practice under the influence of other religions in Canaan. We know this was happening because there are numerous commands warning God's people not to sacrifice their children to Molech, a bronze god furnace whose mechanical arms "reach out" to accept the child placed there. Such parents "profane [God's] holy name" and should be stoned to death, says Leviticus 20:2–5. My mentor said years ago, God *never* requires child sacrifice; only false gods (Molech, et al.) do that. (Even in Abraham's story, Isaac was saved at the last second.)

Some of the Old Testament law is terribly harsh. The instruction about stoning a disobedient child, for example, is found in Deuteronomy 21:18–21. But whatever hardness we find in the Old Testament we must run through the character study of Jesus, because the Bible says if we've seen Jesus, we've seen God. Jesus, whose name Christians claim, fulfilled the old covenant. We are no longer bound by it. (See Matt. 5:17, John 14:9, and Rom. 7:1–3.) We are under a new covenant, in which God's law is written on our hearts. Your child is responsible to hear their own heart; you can't hear it for them.

Child sacrifice is clearly not from the God we see in Jesus. Neither is rejecting your child if they don't turn from their ways or kicking your child out of your home.

I said earlier that 40 percent of homeless youth are LGBTQ. Most of them become homeless the day they come out (or are outed). Kids who are thrown to the streets are approached by a pimp within forty-eight hours. They are usually raped the first night. They are left without any means to protect themselves physically, nor any resources to care for themselves, and selling drugs or their bodies becomes the only possibility they see.

Do you see why I call this child sacrifice?

While conservative churches reach out to face the enormous problem of human trafficking, they are sending their own children into human trafficking. Just to embrace our own children would help address human trafficking.

God gave you parental instincts to love and nurture that little gift of yours. There were no conditions to that. To reject your child requires you to quell those instincts and to steel yourself in cold, hard meanness. Do you seriously think God is asking that of you? How could people think such a thing? I'll tell you: because they think that is how God sees them. That's the truth. They think God is a hard and punishing taskmaster waiting to burn them for any and all infractions. But that is not the God that Jesus shows us. Jesus never gives us one single example or admonition to throw our children out *for any reason*. He shows the prodigal father embracing his son who has not repented at all. Jesus assumes we give our children bread and fish, not stones and snakes, a peaceful home to live in, not soul-crushing rejection and the mean streets.

Remember the story of the man given ten talents in Matthew 25:14–30? *One* talent was worth twenty years' wages. But because he did not trust God, he did not even invest it—he just buried it. God told him he wasted the opportunity given him, and God gave those talents to someone who would steward them wisely. If you reject your child because they are not the child you hoped for and because you don't trust that God's got this, don't be surprised if that child eventually finds a place in another family, with other community, and leaves you far behind.

Instead, fan those parental instincts for all they're worth—the instincts *God* put in you. Only someone terribly, painfully mixed up can really believe that God is asking you to censure your child and *the devil* is the one who wants you to love and nurture them. The Bible says *God* is love and life, and *Satan* is hate and death.

That is God's love you're turning off inside you.

Please, don't let that happen.

FreedHearts Work

Do you still feel you must sacrifice either your child or your faith? Do you believe that's what God wants? Think about ways you've asked your child to mold or bend or diminish into something you could manage or feel okay about. Do you think it's time to relax and let them be who they are? As much as you wanted your parents to let you be who *you* are?

CHAPTER 30

SPEAK THE TRUTH

God has given me the gift of a gay child, and I see that God designed her this way. We are all on the same journey, just in different stages of understanding and allowing God to direct us as we walk this with our children—not our church leaders and church community. Simply just us as parents walking the journey allowing God to direct our thinking and show us love and grace—it's truly all we will ever need.

—Rebecca

This can be a long journey. You may have been rejected, condemned, and judged by people you used to call friends, as well as by your church, and perhaps even by family members. I have been, too.

If you are a Christian parent or family member of an LGBTQ child, I understand. If you are an LGBTQ Christian, I empathize with your pain and struggle. But let me encourage you as I encourage myself: We need to speak the truth, even if our voices shake.

It's fascinating how things get repeated until they become *truth*. To separate the truth out of a swirling mass of repeated thoughts and ideas can be difficult work. I hope you have found some peace with both your child and with God as you seek to love as Christ loved.

I also hope you have a deep conviction that you are on the right side of this issue, the right side of history, and the right side of God's heart. I do.

You may feel conflicted between your community of faith and your child. But the truth is that the conflict is not between your heart and God's heart—the conflict is between your heart and the teaching too many churches have been repeating.

Listen, if God has something to say to you about this, then hear it. Ask God to tell you specifically and *trust the answer.* (And God speaks in still small thoughts, not a big scary voice.) If God convicts your heart, then go with what you hear. If not, then be at peace. Do not try to please the naysayers because you'll never be able to, and you'll only hurt yourself and your family.

To be true to yourself is not a new phenomenon. Shakespeare said four hundred years ago: "To thine own self be true, and it must follow, as the night the day, thou canst not then be false to any man."[1]

And as Paul attributes to God's voice: "Do not be afraid, but speak and do not be silent; for I am with you" (Acts 18:9–10a).

Even if your voice shakes.

FreedHearts Work

Think about what you would say to your family, to the church, to anyone, about what you have discovered already in this process. What would you say about the church's love or failure to love? How has your child and your family suffered pain and loss from another's reaction to your child? What have you discovered about what it means to be community? The most profound thing you can do to change hearts toward LGBTQ people is to tell your story.

PART 5

FINDING A COMMUNITY
OF SUPPORT

CHAPTER 31

YOU NEED SUPPORT TOO

We had already lost church—we weren't ready to lose extended family. I was crushed to realize I couldn't have my church or even my family and affirm my child.

—Liza

Y ou need love, acceptance, peace, comfort, and community, just like your child does. We *all* need these things, but as a parent of a marginalized child, you need to have your wits about you and your feet under you.

You will never find real support as a parent of an LGBTQ child if you remain locked in the closet yourself. The more fully you embrace the life you're actually in—as opposed to the one you had in mind—the more freedom you will find. The more you embrace who your child is—instead of holding out for the one you wish you had—the more beautiful your relationship will be. Your freedom to love and accept your LGBTQ child will help free them to love and accept themselves.

As you embrace your child, you will find yourself in your own process of coming out. We talked earlier about not seeking approval from others, but at some point you will have to say something to your family and to discern which relatives can be supportive and which cannot.

But here are a couple of things to consider.

First, respect your child because this is their story. Second, ask yourself what you hope to get from coming out. Compassionate understanding? Affirmation? Or simply freedom from hiding? All these hopes are valid, but to expect them may set you up to be disappointed.

Picture yourself in your car with the seatbelt on. You reach for something, and the seatbelt grabs you and holds you. The more you lunge forward, the more bound you find yourself. To lean forward in your seatbelt, you must move gently and slowly, so it will give. The same is true in our relationships. The more we lunge at people to get what we want, the more constrained we are. Only as we learn to understand and work with our loved ones will we be free to enjoy them as they are.

Consider these awkward conversations: "Jason still hasn't met that special someone," or "Yes, Sarah still has that same roommate . . . four years later." There is no simple answer for you or for the countless LGBTQ folks who must navigate these situations daily.

You may decide that Aunt Martha, whom you see once a year, doesn't need to know, or you may find allies in surprising places. When Matthew Vines first came out, his parents had a difficult time adjusting, but his grandparents (who'd walked this road before with friends whose son came out) said in complete support, "Well, good for you, Matthew!"

You don't want to tell people who can hurt you by their reaction, but neither do you want to sell people short.

Some people may surprise you, but church friends might disappoint you the most. The support you need is never going to come from the non-affirming church. Why?

Because a non-affirming church is focused on sin, not on Christ. Look at every interaction Jesus had with those the religious leaders rejected. He gave them love, acceptance, peace, comfort, community. That woman at the well, that man born blind, that hemorrhaging woman: they were never going to find comfort in that synagogue with those same religious people who'd rejected them. If they don't have it to give, you can stop going to them for it. Instead, find comfort where they did: in Christ and among the marginalized.

Whatever you do, please don't try to go this road alone. We all need a loving community. Find a PFLAG group, a FreedHearts group, or other affirming community that offers love and encouragement. If the church is not there for you, find community somewhere else.

One family I know reported:

> We lived in a small town when our son came out to us. It was horrible. We wondered how we would ever belong anywhere again. But we finally went to PFLAG (the nearest one was the next town over), and it was like water in the desert. At last, we realized we were not alone. I'm not sure how we would have gotten through it, especially those early months, without those people.

You are not alone, and there are people out there who will offer support. Don't stop looking until you find it.

FreedHearts Work

Talk about your experiences coming out, especially to family. If you have lost family or friends over this, it is a grievous loss. Please, grieve it. Talk about it and journal about it so that you can be free of it. If you need to erect boundaries for people who would hurt you and especially your child, do that. To love someone does not mean to allow yourself to be abused. What new friends have you made or could you still make because of this?

CHAPTER 32

IGNORE THE NAYSAYERS

I'm dealing better with knowing that most of my "friends" here do not share my views now and have distanced themselves from us, because Emily is gay and not ashamed. But what if Emily had not come out? Would I still be there with those friends, judging them like we are judged? I can say now I am thankful for the opportunity to be on the other side.

— Robin

We all seek approval from those around us; people-pleasing starts out as a lifesaver. How would we have survived childhood without learning to gain approval from parents, teachers, and peers? But over time, people-pleasing becomes a curse. Seeking to protect our reputations will cause us to do things we wouldn't otherwise do. In the end, if we try to balance our peers' approval with our children's best interest, we will deeply hurt our children.

Certainly we teach our children not to be swayed by peer pressure. "If everyone were jumping off a bridge, would you, too?" we ask. Yet who is asking us, "If your peer group says homosexuality is wrong, will you, too?" We understand that our kids' intense need for those cool jeans comes from peer pressure. Obviously. But what's not so obvious is that our need to save face to our friends is also peer pressure. Overcoming peer pressure requires as much courage from us as from our kids.

One mom confided to me: "I still live with regret regarding my failures as a parent, and anger is my constant companion because I can't change fast enough. I am crushed that the church *is the driving force* behind treating my son like a second-class citizen." The church's peer pressure machinery steamrolls ahead, unaware of the LGBTQ people they are flattening and the noxious fumes they spread to the entire community. Parents need intense courage to stand up to that.

Our job as a church is to love and encourage each other, but instead, we manage each other's behavior—because of fear. We don't realize that wrestling and working out our own situation in relationship to God is an expected part of the process. It's how we get to know God—and ourselves—better.

Don't let the church direct your process by telling you what's okay and what's not. Christians especially are highly trained to please everyone, from authority figures to fellow believers. God may have allowed such a time as this to set you free from the need to please. God surely did not allow this situation to help you seek further approval of others.

Instead, let God lift your chin and break your need to please (and free your child from that need as well). Let God accomplish profound work in you and your whole family. Just focus on *God*. You'll discover peace, freedom, and joy you never thought possible.

We tend to give our opinion too easily, whether we're asked or not. We simply imagine how we'd feel in that situation, combine it with our best understanding at the time, and offer it up freely. I've been guilty as charged over the years, and I've had to ask forgiveness for my careless advice.

I'll never forget the story I read of a woman who learned she had progressive cancer with a prognosis of just months to live. She became despondent. Her friend said, "If I were you, I'd do lots of things with my kids and put together photo albums for them to remember me by." The woman just looked at her. Really? Is that what you'd do? How do you know what you would do?

Your study group, best friend, or extended family may offer you advice, but unless they're going through a similar situation, their advice is meaningless. Your son or daughter is more important than your friends' approval. While counsel can be indispensable, it can also be crippling. Put others' opinions aside and focus on your child's need. If we can't say in our hearts that our children are more important than others' opinions, it's time to restore our priorities.

We teach our kids to withstand peer pressure; let's agree to do the same.

FreedHearts Work

Think about those things you're reluctant to tell your friends. In what ways have you been less than yourself with others because of what they might think. How have you clipped your own wings? Identify and express that loss. Allow yourself to grieve.

CHAPTER 33

WORDS THAT HURT,
WORDS THAT HEAL

Our pastor started talking about homosexuality. He said, "I'm going to say something that will anger half of you, and then I'll say something that will anger the other half." He forgot all about the things he was saying that HURT people.

— Margot

We used to have a neighbor who could pull off back-handed compliments without even breaking her stride. She would say things like, "Your hair looks good today—*you should fix it more often.*" Or, "That's a cute dress—*is it a little too small?*" I was a preteen, and I just didn't need it.

Words have power to hurt or to heal.

One woman shared with me how her own mother considered her a mistake, telling her when she was just five years old that she'd never wanted her. It took more than thirty years before someone else's words healed that wound.

People say unbelievably hurtful words. Some, like those we addressed in earlier chapters, may seem innocuous or even gracious to those who say them. Others couldn't be considered loving by any stretch of the imagination:

"You're worthless."

"You're a pervert."

"You are disgusting to me."

"You are the spawn of Satan."

"You are going to burn in hell."

"You are a throwaway, and you'll never function in normal society."

You may or may not have experienced similarly hurtful words thrown at you as a parent of an LGBTQ child:

"Does he think he can still be a Christian and be gay?"

"God hates your gay son."

"You really shouldn't talk about it."

"Don't encourage your daughter; she's not worth it."

"Well, you thought wrong; we aren't friends."

"If you love the Church, you'll leave it—for everyone's sake."

Needless to say, a community that tells you things like this is not a supportive community. Just as you are learning to speak healing words to your child—words like "I'm proud of you," "I would never turn you away," "You're my hero," and "You are perfect just the way you are"—you deserve to hear loving, supportive, and healing words as well.

These are some encouraging words said to parents as they support their LGBTQ children:

"You are a good mother, and I see your efforts in raising good boys."

"You are one of the most compassionate people I've ever met."

"I can see God through you."

"You as a mom-figure at the LGBTQ youth center would help a lot of kids—you should volunteer!"

"You are an amazing Christian woman!"

"You don't know it, but other men are watching how you embrace your son. They're inspired by your courage."

"You are a caring soul."

You needn't be ostracized and alone as your child's advocate. There are people out there who are eager to support you as you support your child and who need to see your courage and compassion as well.

FreedHearts Work

Think about the most hurtful thing anyone has ever said to you. Does it still sting? If not, think until you remember one that does. Think of the kindest thing you can remember anyone telling you. Can you feel the power of the difference between the two?

What kind and unkind things have you said? Will you smile at yourself for the kind things and forgive yourself for the unkind things?

CHAPTER 34

DOES YOUR CHURCH
TELL GOOD NEWS . . .
OR BAD NEWS?

*As I was telling my husband about FreedHearts, I paused and
said, "This child was afraid to tell his dad because his dad is a
Christian. How messed up is that?"*

—Carol

When Kyle was considering a new church, he said
to the pastor up front that he wanted to be on the
praise team, told the pastor that he was gay, and asked
if that would be a problem. The pastor said, "Don't say
you're gay; say you're 'struggling with same-sex attraction!' As long as you're struggling, you can be on the praise
team, but as soon as you say you're gay, then you've given
in to it and you can't be on the team."

You see the logic here? As long as you're full of angst
and resistance, you can serve. If you're at peace with who
you are, you're in sin and can't serve. Let's set aside the
ridiculous fallacy that the rest of the praise team—and
leadership—is *not* "in sin." Forget the hypocrisy that only
"non-sinners"—the perfect—are in leadership.

Let's instead look at the more deeply unsettling idea that the true Christian is the angst-ridden person steeped in shame, always looking over their shoulder. That if you are not fighting tooth and nail against who you are at the core, you are not following Christ.

No. That is the *opposite* of the astoundingly good news Jesus brought us when he talked about love, joy, peace, and other fruits of the Holy Spirit. This angst and shame is what the gospel was meant to free us from. I think we've missed the memo. Maybe we just haven't thought this through, but inner turmoil, self-hatred, and soul-splitting is *bad news*—deadly, crushing, demoralizingly bad news.

Jesus did not bring bad news; Jesus brought good news. Astoundingly good news. Hyper-victorious good news! What is that good news? Love. Radical love for all. Love as Jesus described it was to offer a cup of cold water to those who are thirsty; to feed, clothe, and shelter the hungry, naked and homeless; to seek justice for the marginalized. *That* is love.

One mom lamented her church's lack of love, saying: "Our church was going to give out water at the marathon, but they decided not to because some gay people run in the marathon. *Really?*" Does the irony not smack them in the face? These people literally cannot give a cup of water in Christ's name, the very example Christ gave as an *expression* of his love, and they hold that position *in the name of Christ*. It is truly mind-boggling.

If we are not about love, we have missed the point completely. Jesus said people would know we are his followers by our love for each other. So how is it that Christians have come to be known for their . . . um . . . *UNlove?*

Many Christians don't accept this—no one wants to be viewed as unloving. We like to quote Ephesians 4:15 to "speak the truth in love" as permission to challenge someone's choices or "lifestyle," as if our fellow Christians' salvation depends on the truth as we see it. It's like a free pass to tell someone why they are way out of line. But Paul begins Ephesians 4: "I therefore, the prisoner in the Lord, beg you to lead a life worthy of the calling to which you have been called, with all humility and gentleness, with patience, bearing with one another in love."

Calling attention to others' sins (as you define them) is not loving but hateful. To call hate love is simply self-deception.

My friend lived abroad for a while. When American friends visited, sometimes for privacy they would disguise their English by speaking in pig Latin. Once someone asked her, "What language is that?" She said, "It's a form of Latin." Hilarious! And so it is—if by Latin you mean a code that has nothing whatsoever to do with Latin.

To humorously twist the meaning of Latin to include pig Latin is harmless enough. But to twist the meaning of love to include a behavior-management program is terribly harmful and rejects the meaning of love as Jesus defined it.

You do *not* have to compromise your faith in order to love and be loved. And you are not alone. It's your journey, but others are traveling the same road. You can connect with others to find comfort and solidarity. Let's walk together and see the amazing miracles God has ahead.

FreedHearts Work

How are you doing in your church situation? Are you still where you were? Have you moved on to another church? Quit going altogether—if only for a time? Any of those answers are perfectly fine. If you're in the same church, are they completely accepting and affirming of you? Or do you self-edit so that you don't have to hear about it from others?

If you could have it any way you want it, where would you go (or not go) for spiritual community? How would you move forward in your life?

CHAPTER 35

⸻ ⌁ ⸻

THE CHURCH IN CRISIS . . . OR THE CHURCH IN CHRYSALIS?

We finally left our church of fifteen years for an affirming, Jesus-centered church. We had no idea how bound we were by others' opinions until we found a place we're free of them! What surprised us is that we have grown closer to God on this journey than we ever were.

—Mark

A reader emailed me: "My husband and I are looking for a church that will align with our values and accept gays and lesbians. Our current church/denomination 'accepts' them with limits and reservations. Does God only love part of us?? No! My son is gay and a Christian, and we want him to feel free to worship with us at a church that loves him too. Any suggestions for an affirming denomination?"

I recommended she visit www.gaychurch.org for a listing of affirming congregations. While not every affirming church is registered with the site, it's a good place to start. And the tide is turning within many more congregations and denominations, as more and more bodies vote to ordain gay clergy and perform same-sex weddings.

We are, without a doubt, in the throes of a reformation. Not only the entire church as we've known it but the surrounding culture is reforming and changing. Change brings bountiful opportunity, but it also disrupts. The more you like things battened down, the more terrifying change can be. When change looms, we often cling all the harder to the old ways: *if we could just go back to how things used to be*. But the old ways that got us to this point will not move us forward. As logical as it may sound to "go back to the Bible" to fix our woes, that will not be the answer. Women barefoot and pregnant, blacks as slaves, LGBTQ people in the closet or prison: those are all relics of the past, *not* "good old days" to which we can return if we wish hard enough.

The late author and scholar Phyllis Tickle described it this way:

> Every 500 years we go through a time of great upheaval when everything changes—intellectually, politically, culturally, sociologically. Five hundred years ago we called it the Great Reformation, a thousand years ago it was the Great Schism, 1,500 years ago it was the Great Decline and Fall, and 2,000 years ago it was the Great Transition. Today, what we are experiencing has been called the Great Emergence. As in every transition before it, there has been such an abrupt interruption in the way things are that there's no going back.[1]

The church may appear to be in crisis. But what if the church is in chrysalis? To say *crisis* is to seek a way back; to say *chrysalis* is to seek a way forward.

When a caterpillar goes through chrysalis to become a butterfly, it doesn't mess around. It must enter a cocoon and completely liquefy for the transformation to occur. No chrysalis, no transformation. Or, no death, no resurrection.

The church you see transforming before your eyes is *not* because God has lost hold of the universe and Satan has taken over—no matter how many good people hold on to old ways for dear life, no matter how many evangelists scream from the pulpit.

God is the one affecting change in the world and in the church.

People are leaving non-affirming churches and joining affirming churches because that is where the Spirit is moving. Our culture—the one God is still very much involved in—is moving from *rule*-based faith into *love*-based faith. We are seeking to become more aligned with the relationship focus Jesus showed us. That dissonance with the rule-focused church is the Spirit's work. It is not disobedience on your part; it is not a loss of control and we must get it together and rein it all back in. It won't go back in.

You and the LGBTQ community are a vibrant move of God in the church today. Do you believe that God was distracted when your child discovered they were gay, and now you must scamper around and fix it all? Or do you believe that God gave you that child on purpose because God is shifting the focus of the church?

You are not alone. Others are traveling the same road. You can connect with us to find comfort and solidarity. Let's walk together and see the amazing miracles God has ahead.

FreedHearts Work

The evidence of the Holy Spirit's work is love, joy, peace, patience, kindness, generosity, faithfulness, gentleness, and self-control. Where do you see these "fruits of the spirit" (Gal. 5:22–23) in the church today? Are they blossoming more in certain places than others?

Is it exciting (even if scary) to be part of that movement?

CHAPTER 36

YOUR KID WILL BE FINE

I remember the first time I felt perfect peace return to me (a feeling I had known prior to my son coming out, before the turmoil within me began). The perfect peace returned to me the moment I thanked God for my son being gay.

—Sara

Whoever you are, wherever you are on this journey, please remember—it's *your* journey.

There is no one right way—and there is no one right time frame. Wherever you are, you are doing just fine, and there are better days ahead.

It's your life. It's your child. It's your journey. Don't let anyone make you feel bad for wherever you are in this difficult process. They are wrong and you are right, because love is always right (1 John 4:20).

And never, ever let anyone make you feel bad or ashamed for simply loving and accepting your child or for wanting unconditional love from your parents and family.

Fully embrace the child God has given you and take comfort in these thoughts:

Your child is gay. Don't be afraid; it's going to be all right. In fact, it will be amazing.

Your world feels shaky, but I encourage you to relax.
    It won't just be okay; it will be better than okay.
Your child is gay, or bi, or trans, but that's not all —
    your child is so much more.
Your child is courageous to follow their heart in the
    face of incredible condemnation.
Your child is daring to be who they are in the face of fear.
Your child is brave to tell you the truth in the face of
    possible rejection.
Your child is strong to stand on the truth of their heart.
Your child is dependent on God to care for their life,
    but independent enough not to cower down to
    societal pressure.
Your child has a deep desire to love and be loved in a
    world that has devalued love.
Your child is an original in a world of phonies who
    hide who they are.
Your child is honest and desires to live life as the
    person God created them to be.
Your child is an inspiration to their friends and to me,
    and they can be an inspiration to you as well.
Your child is gay, but that's not everything they
    are. They are courageous, daring, brave, strong,
    dependent and independent, loving, original,
    honest, and an inspiration.
Be proud. Rejoice. You've raised a great kid.

FreedHearts Work

Go and express your joy and love for your child. As much
as you're able, tell them you're proud of them, that you're
grateful for them, that you wouldn't want them to be any
other way. If that's not yet true, allow yourself to move
toward that and say as much as *is* true!

APPENDIX

Letter to a Community

This father shared a letter he wrote that beautifully expresses our duty as parents to embrace and protect our children.

Dear family and friends:

When you are faced with a big turn you never anticipated, your first reaction is shock. Other emotions quickly follow, like anger, denial, and shame. You consider your life and wonder, "What could I have done differently?" Or worse, "What are people going to say about me?" Finally you say, "I can't live like this anymore, I can't fix things to make everyone happy, but I can tell the truth." That is where I am.

My dearly loved daughter Suzanne is gay.

You can understand the difficulty of dealing with this news—for Suzanne, Debbie and me, our other daughters, family, church friends, work friends, and the community. Everyone says, "This is what I would do." Well, until you are in this position, you really don't know what you would do.

I know the verses in Genesis 19, Leviticus 18 and 20, Romans 1, 1 Corinthians 6, and 1 Timothy 1—no one need remind me. But because I've never personally struggled with this, I used those verses only to judge and condemn others. I never considered how those who were burdened with this were struggling to reconcile these words with their faith. God have mercy on me. Now I do. I would never try to change your convictions. I do ask that you act from love, whatever your convictions. Pray. Please do not approach gay people with condemnation and scripture. Approach them with prayer and love—to do so is not to shirk your Christian duties but, on the contrary, *it is to carry your Christian duties out.* It is to be like Christ. Remember Jesus' compassion for those considered the worst of sinners in the Jewish world (prostitutes and extorters). Modern-day imitators of Jesus need to be known for their love instead of their judgment. God alone will do the judging. (Whether you rejoice in that fact or shed a tear may reveal much about your heart.)

Faith is personal, and no one can command it. God gave me free will, and so as a father, I must give my children free will. I cannot tell them what to think but encourage them to seek God for themselves, as I always have.

Instead of offering counsel, I ask you to pray for us all, don't spread rumors. We have confided in few, so few know the dynamics of this in our family. Listen only to what you hear directly from us.

Nothing has changed between my daughter and me; I remain an active father in her life, and I love her and would lay down my life for her.

May God bless you all and please keep Debbie, Suzanne, Beth, and Lauren in your prayers.

—Nathan

Letter to a Daughter

A letter from a grandfather to his daughter regarding his grandson[1]. This letter may sound harsh, but I include it because it turns the tables, as Jesus turned the tables on the Pharisees who demanded "righteousness" of others, blind to their own glaring judgment. (Matt. 23)

Dear Christine:

I'm disappointed in you as a daughter. You're correct that we have a "shame in the family" but mistaken about what it is. Kicking Chad out of your home simply because he told you he was gay is the real "abomination" here. A parent disowning her child is what goes "against nature." The only intelligent thing I heard you saying in all this was that "you didn't raise your son to be gay." Of course you didn't. He was born this way and didn't choose it any more than he chose being left-handed. You, however, have made a choice of being hurtful, narrow-minded and backward. So, while we are in the business of disowning our children, I think I'll take this moment to say goodbye to you. I now have a fabulous (as the gays put it) grandson to raise, and I don't have time for a heartless B–word of a daughter.

If you find your heart, give us a call.

—Dad

Letter to an LGBTQ Child

A letter from a dad to his child.

I am so sorry. And I am so thankful.

First, please let me say that it is an honor and a

privilege to be your parent. I could not have asked for a better child.

I am sorry if I ever did or said anything, or failed to do or say something to let you know how much I love and accept you. I am also so very sorry for the hurt and rejection and condemnation you have felt from some of our family members, those you considered to be friends, and from the church. On behalf of my family and my church, I apologize from the deepest places of my heart. I am thankful that through this journey you have deepened your relationship with God as you have come to know and experience unconditional love and grace.

I am thankful that you have discovered that the truth of Jesus is very different from the truth of most of today's evangelical churches.

I am thankful that you have come to know the truth about God's heart for you.

I am thankful for the love that many of your family, and your true friends—old and new—have shown you.

And I am thankful that you have found a church and fellow Christians who love you as Christ loved them.

Most of all, I am thankful for you. You are an amazing child. I would not change anything about you. There is nothing you can ever do to disappoint me.

I will always love you. I will always be your advocate and celebrate your life.

I will always be your biggest fan.

—Dad

Letter to a Family

Dear Family:

Having just finished college and begun the transition into

adult life, I am reflecting on those who have influenced me and helped shape me into the person I have become. Chief on that list is my creator, God, followed by you, my family. There's an old saying "it takes a village to raise a child," and you, my family, have been my village. I am writing to say thank you. Also I write to invite you to know better the person I am, to share life together with greater authenticity and communion.

I am gay. I have known since my early adolescent years that I did not share the same growing attractions my peers were experiencing but for fear of being different, I convinced myself that I was just like everyone else. I did not really admit to myself that I was attracted to other men until high school. At that point, it became a crisis of faith. My family upbringing taught me that God loves all of his children and requires only faith to benefit from His grace, but at the same time, my church expressed condemnation towards those of a homosexual orientation. In a leap of faith, I spoke to a Christian mentor about my "problem," and he led me onto a path of change through prayer, accountability, and self-discipline.

At first, this struggle to change was invigorating and injected new life into my still juvenile faith. I was discovering the transformative power of God and making decisions to align my life and will with His, so that Christ could live and minister through me more effectively. But as years wore on with little or no sign of real transformation, I grew less and less convinced that aligning myself with God's will required me to become straight.

A crucial turning point came as my relationship with my college girlfriend ended. I had prayed and waited patiently through two years of our relationship for God to enact the transformation in me that would allow me to commit myself to her in a proposal of marriage, but that change never came. As much as I loved her, I grew to realize that I could only ever love her as a close friend. I would never be able to love her in all the ways she deserved. As hard as it was, I realized that I had to let her go, to free her to find the love that I could never offer her. That marked the beginning of a journey of discernment that brought me face-to-face with God in a way I had never before experienced.

I knew God had led me to a place of self-acceptance, but I didn't know what that meant for my hopes, my dreams, or my future. I wanted to know God's will, so I began to study the process of discernment, to learn how godly people throughout history have discerned the will of their Creator. As part of that process, I surrendered my hopes, fears, dreams, desires, and preconceived notions, laying them before God and opening my heart to the scriptures in prayer and study. Throughout those months, I have grown comfortable with a reading of scripture that frees me to accept myself, to love as it comes naturally to me, and to continue my walk as a gay Christian.

There is obviously much more to my story, including my understanding of God's word on sexuality, and I would be glad to share any of that with you. This letter serves simply as an invitation to begin that conversation, to know me more deeply and to live more authentically as a family.

Sincerely,
—Ben Shopland

The Robertsons' Story

"Mom, I'm gay." Earth-shattering words to many conservative Christian parents—tragically, many view it as right up there with, "Your child has a brain tumor." Actually, Christians will empathize with a brain tumor, but just try telling the church your child is gay and you will find the limit of grace withheld not only from gay Christians but from their accepting families. Not only what is said but unsaid can be oppressive for a family seeking love and truth.

I do not blame the parents in these situations for one nanosecond. Lord knows, they are trying to respond, with the wind knocked out of them, in an area where the church at large allows no breathing room. Parents blame themselves and Christians blame them. Seriously. No sooner do we hear the word gay or lesbian than we brace for impact—because we know the attack is coming.

This story was posted on Facebook. My daughter went to school with his brother. The mother, Linda, gave me kind permission to post this in the hope of impacting lives and preventing tragedy. This is why our response as a Christian community matters. A real person with a real story.

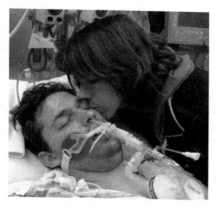

photo: Linda and Ryan Robertson

Just Because He Breathes

On the night of November 20, 2001, a conversation held over Instant Messenger changed our lives forever. Our twelve-year-old son messaged me in my office from the computer in his bedroom.

Ryan says: can i tell u something

Mom says: Yes I am listening

Ryan says: well i don't know how to say this really but, well . . ., i can't keep lying to you about myself. I have been hiding this for too long and i sorta have to tell u now. By now u probably have an idea of what i am about to say.

Ryan says: I am gay

Ryan says: i can't believe i just told you

Mom says: Are you joking?

Ryan says: no

Ryan says: i thought you would understand because of uncle don

Mom says: of course I would

Mom says: but what makes you think you are?

Ryan says: i know i am

Ryan says: i don't like hannah

Ryan says: it's just a cover-up

Mom says: but that doesn't make you gay . . .

Ryan says: i know

Ryan says: but u don't understand

Ryan says: i am gay

Mom says: tell me more

Ryan says: it's just the way i am and it's something i know

Ryan says: u r not a lesbian and u know that it is the
same thing

Mom says: what do you mean?

Ryan says: i am just gay

Ryan says: i am that

Mom says: I love you no matter what

Ryan says: i am white not black

Ryan says: i know

Ryan says: i am a boy not a girl

Ryan says: i am attracted to boys not girls

Ryan says: u know that about yourself and i know this

Mom says: what about what God thinks about acting
on these desires?

Ryan says: i know

Mom says: thank you for telling me

Ryan says: and i am very confused about that right now

Mom says: I love you more for being honest

Ryan says: i know

Ryan says: thanx

We were completely shocked. Not that we didn't know
and love gay people—my only brother had come out to
us several years before, and we adored him. But Ryan?

He was unafraid of anything, tough as nails, and *all* boy. We had not seen this coming, and the emotion that overwhelmed us, kept us awake at night and, sadly, influenced all of our reactions over the next six years, was *fear*.

We said all the things that we thought loving Christian parents who believed the Bible to be the Word of God should say:

> We love you. We will *always* love you. And this is hard. *Really* hard. But we know what God says about this, and so you are going to have to make some really difficult choices.
>
> We love you. But there are other men who have faced this same struggle, and God has worked in them to change their desires. We'll get you their books . . . you can listen to their testimonies. And we will trust God with this.
>
> We love you. But you are young, and your sexual orientation is still developing. The feelings you've had for other guys don't make you gay. So please don't tell anyone that you *are* gay. You don't know who you are yet. Your identity is not that you are gay—it is that you are a child of God.
>
> We love you. We will *always* love you. But if you are going to follow Jesus, holiness is your only option. You are going to have to choose to follow Jesus, no matter what. And since you know what the Bible says, and since you want to follow God, embracing your sexuality is *not* an option.

Basically, we told our son that he had to choose between Jesus and his sexuality. We forced him to make a choice between God and being a sexual person. Choosing God, practically, meant living a lifetime of loneliness (never to fall in love, have his first kiss, hold hands, share intimacy companionship, experience romance), but it also meant the abundant life, perfect peace and eternal rewards. So, for the first six years, he tried to choose Jesus. Like so many others before him, he pleaded with God to help him be attracted to girls. He memorized Scripture, met with his youth pastor weekly, enthusiastically participated in all the church youth group events and Bible studies, got baptized, read all the books that claimed to know where his gay feelings came from, dove into counseling to further discover the "why's" of his unwanted attraction to other guys, worked through painful conflict resolution with my husband and I, and built strong friendships with other guys—straight guys—just like he was told to. He even came out to his entire youth group, giving his testimony of how God had rescued him from the traps of the enemy, and sharing—by memory—verse after verse that God had used to draw Ryan to himself.

But nothing changed. God didn't answer his prayer—or ours—though we were all believing with faith that the God of the Universe—the God for whom *nothing* is impossible—could easily make Ryan straight. But he did not.

Though our hearts may have been good (we truly thought what we were doing was loving), we did not even give Ryan a chance to wrestle with God, to figure out what *he* believed God was telling him through Scripture about his sexuality. We had believed firmly in giving each of our four children the space to question Christianity, to decide for themselves if they wanted to follow Jesus, to truly *own* their own faith. But we were too afraid to give Ryan that room when it came to his sexuality, for fear that he'd make the wrong choice.

And so, just before his eighteenth birthday, Ryan, depressed, suicidal, disillusioned and convinced that he would never be able to be loved by God, made a new choice. He decided to throw out his Bible and his faith at the same time, and to try searching for what he desperately wanted—peace—another way. And the way he chose to try first was drugs.

We had—unintentionally—taught Ryan to hate his sexuality. And since sexuality cannot be separated from the self, we had taught Ryan to hate himself. So as he began to use drugs, he did so with a recklessness and a lack of caution for his own safety that was alarming to everyone who knew him.

Suddenly our fear of Ryan someday having a boyfriend (a possibility that honestly terrified me) seemed trivial in contrast to our fear of Ryan's death, especially in light of his recent rejection of Christianity, and his mounting anger at God.

Ryan started with weed and beer . . . but in six short months was using cocaine, crack and heroin. He was hooked from the beginning, and his self-loathing and rage at God only fueled his addiction. Shortly after, we lost contact with him. For the next year-and-a-half we didn't know where he was, or even if he was dead or alive. And during that horrific time, God had our full attention. We stopped praying for Ryan to become straight. We started praying for him to know that God loved him. We stopped praying for him never to have a boyfriend. We started praying that someday he'd come back to Jesus. We even stopped praying for him to come home to us . . . we only wanted him to come home to God.

By the time our son called us, after 18 long months of silence, God had completely changed our perspective. Because Ryan had done some pretty terrible things while using drugs, the first thing he asked me was this:

Do you think you can ever forgive me? (I told him of course, he was already forgiven. He had *always* been forgiven.)

Do you think you could ever love me again? (I told him that we had never stopped loving him, not for one second. We loved him then more than we had ever loved him.)

Do you think you could even love me with a boyfriend?

(Crying, I told him that we could love him with fifteen boyfriends. We just wanted him back in our lives. We just wanted to have a relationship with him again . . . *and* with his boyfriend.)

And a new journey was begun. One of healing, restoration, open communication and grace. LOTS of grace. And God was present every step of the way, leading and guiding us, gently reminding us simply to love our son, and leave the rest up to Him.

Over the next ten months, we learned to love our son. Period. No buts. No conditions. Just because he breathes. We learned to love whoever our son loved. And it was easy. What I had been so afraid of became a blessing. The journey wasn't without mistakes, but we had grace for each other, and the language of apology and forgiveness became a natural part of our relationship. As our son pursued recovery from drug and alcohol addiction, we pursued him. God taught us how to love him, to rejoice over him, to be proud of the man he was becoming. We were all healing . . . and most importantly, Ryan began to think that if *we* could forgive him and love him, then maybe God could, too.

And then Ryan made the classic mistake of a recovering addict . . . he got back together with his old friends . . . his using friends. And one evening that was supposed to simply be a night at the movies turned out to be the first time he had shot up in ten months . . . and the last time. Ryan died on July 16, 2009. And we lost the ability to love our gay son . . . because we no longer had a gay son. What we had wished for . . . prayed for . . . hoped for . . . that we would *not* have a gay son, came true. But not at all in the way we used to envision.

Now, when I think back on the fear that governed all my reactions during those first six years after Ryan told us he was gay, I cringe as I realize how foolish I was. I was afraid of all the wrong things. And I grieve, not only for my oldest son, who I will miss every day for the rest of my life, but for the mistakes I made. I grieve for what could have been, had we been walking by *faith* instead of by *fear*. Now, whenever Rob and I join our gay friends for an evening, I think about how much I would love to be visiting with Ryan and his partner over dinner. But instead, we visit Ryan's gravestone. We celebrate anniversaries: the would-have-been birthdays and the unforgettable day of his death. We wear orange—his color. We hoard memories: pictures, clothing he wore, handwritten notes, lists of things he loved, tokens of his passions, recollections of the funny songs he invented, his Curious George and baseball blankey, anything, really, that reminds us of our beautiful boy . . . for that is all we have left, and there will be no new memories. We rejoice in our adult children, and in our growing family as they marry . . . but ache for the one of our "gang of four" who is missing. We mark life by the days BC (before coma) and AD (after death), because we are different people now; our life was irrevocably changed—in a million ways—by his death. We treasure friendships with others who "get it" . . . because they, too, have lost a child.

We weep. We seek heaven for grace and mercy and redemption as we try—not to get better but to be better. And we pray that God can somehow use our story to help other parents learn to truly love their children. Just because they breathe.

Linda Diane Robertson,
robertson.family@frontier.com
Written on December 5, 2012
Posted on January 14, 2013 –
Ryan's would-have-been-24th birthday
JustBecauseHeBreathes.com

NOTES

Chapter 6: "Praying Away" the Gay—the Impossible Dream

1. Linda Robertson, JustBecauseHeBreathes.com.

2. Lisa Ling, "Special Report: God and Gays," *Our America with Lisa Ling*, YouTube video, June 20, 2013, https://www.youtube.com/watch?v=li0dz7oYVIU.

Chapter 7: Hoping for Change Can Hurt

1. Josh Krueger McAdams, "Ex-gay Panel Discussion with Alan Chambers," YouTube video from a Gay Christian Network Conference, Orlando, FL, January 6, 2012, http://www.youtube.com/watch?v=TXgA7_QRvhg.

2. Alan Chambers, "Alan Chamber's Full Apology to Members of the LGBTQ Community," Speak.Love.Org, June 19, 2013, http://wespeaklove.org/exodus/.

Chapter 9: Terrified to Tell You

1. L. E. Durso and G. J. Gates, "Serving Our Youth: Findings from a National Survey of Service Providers Working with Lesbian, Gay, Bisexual, and Transgender Youth Who Are Homeless or at Risk of Becoming Homeless" (Los Angeles: The Williams Institute with

True Colors Fund and The Palette Fund, June 2013, from http://williamsinstitute.law.ucla.edu/wp-content/uploads/Durso-Gates-LGBT-Homeless-Youth-Survey-July-2012.pdf.

Chapter 11: What Not to Say, Part 2

1. This story is strongly associated with the apostle John, but it is not present in the earliest manuscripts. It may well have come from Jesus through oral tradition—it certainly sounds like him.

Chapter 12: Beyond the Binary

1. Benjamin L. Corey, "If God Only Made Male & Female, What about Intersex," *Patheos* (blog), August 21, 2015, http://www.patheos.com/blogs/formerlyfundie/if-god-only-made-male-female-what-about-intersex/.

2. Intersex Society of North America, "What Is Intersex?" http://www.isna.org/faq/what_is_intersex.

3. Megan K. DeFranza, *Sex Difference in Christian Theology: Male, Female, and Intersex in the Image of God* (Grand Rapids: Eerdmans, 2015).

4. Alice Dreger, "Is Anatomy Destiny?" *TED Talks*, filmed December 2010, http://www.ted.com/talks/alice_dreger_is_anatomy_destiny?language=en.

Chapter 13: "He's Wearing a Dress!"

1. National Center for Transgender Equality, "Understanding Transgender: Frequently Asked Questions about Transgender People," http://transequality.org/Resources/NCTE_UnderstandingTrans.pdf.

2. Susan Page, "Understanding Gender Nonconforming Children," *The Diane Rehm Show*, National Public Radio, September 5, 2013, http://thedianerehmshow.org/shows/2013-09-05/understanding-gender-nonconforming-children/.

Chapter 14: The Masculinity Myth

1. Brené Brown, "Listening to Shame," *TED Talks*, filmed March 16, 2012, http://www.ted.com/talks/brene_brown_listening_to_shame?language=er.

Chapter 15: Embrace Your Child

1. Tony Campolo, *Stories That Feed Your Soul* (Ventura, CA: Regal, 2010), 186–87.

Chapter 17: Don't Shame Your Child

1. Brené Brown, *Daring Greatly: How the Courage to Be Vulnerable Transforms the Way We Live, Love, Parent, and Lead* (New York: Gotham Books, 2012).

Chapter 19: Surrender Control

1. Susan Cottrell, *How Not to Lose Your Teen: Raising Kids Who Love God and You Too* (Austin, TX: FreedHearts, Inc., 2013).

Chapter 24: God's Got This

1. See "Just Because He Breathes" in the appendix.

Chapter 25: The Ultimate Fear: Hell

1. Tentmaker.org, Hell. See also Crystal St. Marie Lewis, *Quenched: What Everybody (Especially Christians) Should Know about Hell* (Amazon Digital Services LLC, 2012).

2. Benjamin L. Corey, "What Jesus Talked about When He Talked about Hell," *Patheos* (blog), June 25, 2014, http://www.patheos.com/blogs/formerlyfundie/what-jesus-talked-about-when-he-talked-about-hell/.

Chapter 27: The "Clobber Passages" (Old Testament)

1. Adele Berlin, *The JPS Commentary: Esther* (Philadelphia: Jewish Publication Society, 2001), xviii.

2. Ibid., 55.

3. "Terminology of Homosexuality," Wikipedia, last modified March 31, 2016, https://en.wikipedia.org/wiki/Terminology_of_homosexuality.

4. Brent Pickett, "Homosexuality," in *The Stanford Encyclopedia of Philosophy* (Fall 2015), Edward N. Zalta, ed., http://plato.stanford.edu/archives/fall2015/entries/homosexuality/.

Chapter 28: The "Clobber Passages" (New Testament)

1. Matthew Vines, *God and the Gay Christian* (New York: Convergent Books 2014), 121.
2. Ibid., 125.

Chapter 30: Speak the Truth

1. William Shakespeare, *Hamlet*, 1.3.78–80.

Chapter 35: The Church in Crisis . . . or the Church in Chrysalis?

1. Karen Hilfman Millson, "Interview with Phyllis Tickle," *The UC Observer*, December 2012, http://www.ucobserver.org/interviews/2012/12/interview_phyllis_tickle/.

Appendix

1. Mark Molloy, "Grandfather Writes Scathing Letter to Homophobic Daughter for Disowning Gay Son," Metro.co.uk, http://metro.co.uk/2013/10/03/fckh8-grandfather-blasts-daughter-in-letter-for-disowning-gay-son-4132743/.